Give It Back!

Kimberly Daniels

A STRANG COMPANY

Most Strang Communications/Charisma House/Siloam/FrontLine/Realms products are available at special quantity discounts for bulk purchase for sales promotions, premiums, fund-raising, and educational needs. For details, write Strang Communications/Charisma House/Siloam/FrontLine/Realms, 600 Rinehart Road, Lake Mary, Florida 32746, or telephone (407) 333-0600.

Give It Back! by Kimberly Daniels
Published by Charisma House
A Strang Company
600 Rinehart Road
Lake Mary, Florida 32746
www.charismahouse.com

Unless otherwise noted, all Scripture quotations are from New King James Version of the Bible. Copyright © 1979, 1980, 1982 by Thomas Nelson, Inc., publishers. Used by permission.

Scripture quotations marked AMP are from the Amplified Bible. Old Testament copyright © 1965, 1987 by the Zondervan Corporation. The Amplified New Testament copyright © 1954, 1958, 1987 by the Lockman Foundation. Used by permission.

Scripture quotations marked KJV are from the King James Version of the Bible.

Cover design by Bill Johnson
Author photos: Reggie Anderson Photography, www.reggiephotos4u.com

Library of Congress Cataloging-in-Publication Data

Daniels, Kimberly.
  Give it back! / Kimberly Daniels.
     p. cm.
  Includes bibliographical references.
  ISBN-13: 978-1-59979-057-2 (trade paper) 1. Spiritual warfare. I. Title.

  BV4509.5.D245 2007
  235'.4--dc22

2006030246

First Edition

07 08 09 10 11— 987654321
Printed in the United States of America

Contents

Dedication

I DEDICATE THIS BOOK to the greatest country in the world—America! We need a fresh wind of revival within our borders. True revival is only birthed out of the loins of intercession. The Spirit of the Lord is raising the standard for prayer in America. The enemy has come into America like a flood, but God Himself is dressed for battle on the behalf of His bride. America, hear the word of the Lord from Isaiah 59:

> Behold, the Lord's hand is not shortened at all, that it cannot save, nor His ear dull with deafness; that it cannot hear. But your iniquities have made a separation between you and your God, and your sins have hidden His face from you, so that He will not hear. For your hands are defiled with blood and your fingers with iniquity; your lips have spoken lies, your tongue mutters wickedness.
>
> None sues or calls in righteousness [but for the sake of doing injury to others—to take some undue advantage]; no one goes to law honestly and pleads [his case] in truth; they trust in emptiness, worthlessness and futility, and speaking lies! They conceive mischief and bring forth evil! They hatch adder's eggs and weave the spider's web; he who eats of their eggs dies, and [from an egg] which is crushed a viper breaks out [for their nature is ruinous, deadly, evil].
>
> Their webs will not serve as clothing, nor will they cover themselves with what they make; their works are works of iniquity, and the act of violence is in their hands. Their feet run to

evil, and they make haste to shed innocent blood. Their thoughts
are thoughts of iniquity; desolation and destruction are in their
paths and highways. The way of peace they know not, and there
is no justice or right in their goings. They have made them into
crooked paths; whoever goes in them does not know peace.

Therefore are justice and right far from us, and righteousness
and salvation do not overtake us. We expectantly wait for light,
but [only] see darkness; for brightness, but we walk in obscurity
and gloom. We grope for the wall like the blind, yes, we grope
like those who have no eyes. We stumble at noonday as in the
twilight; in dark places and among those who are full of life and
vigor, we are as dead men. We all groan and growl like bears and
moan plaintively like doves. We look for justice, but there is
none; for salvation, but it is far from us.

For our transgressions are multiplied before You [O Lord],
and our sins testify against us; for our transgressions are with
us, and as for our iniquities, we know and recognize them [as]:
Rebelling against and denying the Lord, turning away from
following our God, speaking oppression and revolt, conceiv-
ing in and muttering and moaning from the heart words of
falsehood.

Justice is turned away backward, and righteousness (uprightness and right standing with God) stands far off; for truth has
fallen in the streets (the city's forum), and uprightness cannot
enter [the courts of justice]. Yes, truth is lacking, and he who
departs from evil makes himself a prey. And the Lord saw it, and
it displeased Him that there was no justice. And He saw that
there was no man and wondered that *there was no intercessor* [no
one to intervene on the behalf of truth and right]; therefore His
own arm brought Him victory, and His own righteousness [hav-
ing the Spirit without measure] sustained Him.

For [the Lord] put on righteousness as a breastplate or coat
of mail, and salvation as a helmet upon His head; He put on
garments of vengeance for clothing and was clad with zeal [and
furious divine jealousy] as a cloak. According as their deeds
deserve, so will He repay wrath to His adversaries, recompense
to His enemies; on the foreign islands and coastlands He will

make compensation. So [as a result of the Messiah's intervention] they shall [reverently] fear the name of the Lord from the west, and His glory from the rising of the sun. When the enemy shall come in like a flood, the Spirit of the Lord will lift up a standard against him and put him to flight [for He will come like a rushing stream which the breath of the Lord drives].

He shall come as a Redeemer to Zion and those in Jacob (Israel) who turn from transgression, says the Lord. As for Me, this is My covenant or league with them, says the Lord: My Spirit, Who is upon you [and Who writes the law of God inwardly on the heart], and My words which I have put in your mouth shall not depart out of your mouth, or out of the mouths of your [true, spiritual] children, or out of the mouths of your children's children, says the Lord, from henceforth and forever.

—ISAIAH 59:1–21, AMP, EMPHASIS ADDED

This scripture says that there was no intercessors to intervene on the behalf of what was right. I know that this book will stir up intercessors around the world, but I dedicate it to be a clarion call to prayer warriors within the borders of America. Gird your loins, mount up, and move forward against the antichrist spirits that rule over our nation. Confront the enemy and take back what he has stolen from God's people. Shout the battle cry: "Give it back!" Send the message to the enemy: "You're going down!" No longer will he have dominion over America. Our land will be healed!

Where does healing begin? Repentance! I am writing this dedication on July 14, 2006 (7/14/06). I do not think that this is a coincidence. Read 2 Chronicles 7:14 (KJV) aloud, noting the emphasis I added, and begin to repent for corporate national sin.

If my people, which are called by my name, shall humble themselves, and pray, and seek my face, and turn from their wicked ways [repent]; *then* will I hear from heaven, and will forgive their sin, and *will heal their land.*

The following scriptures continue by showing the result of that repentance. Read these verses as a promise for the repentance of America.

> Now mine eyes shall be open, and mine ears attent unto the prayer that is made in this place [America]. For now have I chosen and sanctified this house, that my name may be there for ever: and mine eyes and mine heart shall be there perpetually. And as for thee, if thou will walk before me, as David thy father walked, and do according to all that I have commanded thee, and shalt observe my statutes and my judgments; then will I stablish the throne of thy kingdom, according as I have covenanted with David thy father, saying, There shall not fail thee a man to be ruler in Israel.
> —2 CHRONICLES 7:15–18, KJV

Now note the result of a lack of repentance on the part of America:

> But if ye turn away, and forsake my statutes and my commandments, which I have set before you, and shall go and serve other gods, and worship them; then will I pluck them up by the roots out of my land which I have given them; and this house, which I have sanctified for my name, will I cast out of my sight, and will make it to be a proverb and a byword among all nations.
> —2 CHRONICLES 7:19–20, KJV

The scriptures above say it all. We know what our national sins are in America! Our iniquities have separated us from our God, and our prayers have been hindered. The good news is that the Messiah Himself is intervening. America is coming under an open heaven that has been closed in the past because of corporate national sin. Justice is coming forward, and righteousness is nigh us. No longer shall truth fall in our city's forum. God is placing the called-out ones in positions of political influence that have influence in the spirit. It is already done—we must take over the airways in the spirit and the polls in the natural.

Natural and spiritual authority is forming a chain that will bind up the powers of those who hate God. No longer shall they rule in high places in America. God is releasing spiritual Hezekiahs who will tear the high places down and restore what the locusts have devoured! This restoration will spread to other countries as America is revived. America is the spearhead of the nations!

As we turn from our wicked ways and come out of obscurity concerning the things of the gospel, it will have a domino effect on the world. Let it begin in Florida, the first coast where prayers were prayed in America! And as the prophets have spoken, I confirm: Florida is the key to reformation in America! Doors are opening in the spirit to restore our spiritual legacy. Because the roots of America are holy, the fruits shall be holy. The systems of this world that defy the Most High are coming down!

Please pray with me:

> *Father God, in the name of Jesus, we draw from the anointing of the blood of the martyrs who prayed the first prayers in our country. As their blood cries from the ground, we open our ears to hear the clarion call. We get in place to restore that which human secularists have stolen from our midst. In the name of Jesus, I dedicate this book to:*

- *Prayer being restored in our public schools.*

- *The overturn of* Roe v. Wade *so that legal innocent bloodshed will cease in America and the standard will spread to other countries.*

- *Making all same-sex marriages, civil unions, and domestic partnerships illegal from the lowest levels of government to the top.*

- *Righteousness being restored to our justice system.*

- *Dealing with the corruption in our criminal justice system.*

- *Godly men and women being strategically placed in key political positions in our government.*

Amen.

There are powerful principles in this book. I pray that as you read it, you will gird up and get on the wall to pray things that are significant to the kingdom of God. Remember, if you seek the things of the kingdom first, God will take care of your personal needs. Gird up your loins and mount up for war—there is a battle cry being released over America! The forces of the Lord are marching in synchronization. They are coming out of the old wineskins of passivity and stepping into a new cadence of greater authority in the Spirit that will manifest in the natural. If I were you, I would not be left behind.

—Apostle Kim

Foreword

IFIRST BECAME INVOLVED in spiritual warfare through deliverance in the 1980s. During the 1990s God was gracious to give us more understanding of this important subject. It was during this time that I met Kim Daniels. Her hatred of evil and her desire to set people free have been consistent throughout. God has continued to upgrade her understanding of the spirit realm, and this book is a must for those wanting to be more effective in spiritual warfare.

Kim has become an authority on the subjects of deliverance and spiritual warfare. She has studied and researched the material in this book with a depth that few others have achieved. She is a voice that is calling Zion to arise and shine. She is challenging the church to a new level of deliverance and warfare.

Kim Daniels has a hatred for witchcraft and the works of darkness. She does not write to exalt the enemy but to expose him. You cannot be effective against the enemy unless you hate iniquity and the evil works of demons and fallen angels. We must hate the enemy with a perfect hatred. (See Psalm 139:21–22.)

Some of the material will be new to readers. The apostolic anointing has a pioneering grace. We need pioneers to take us into new truth and territory. God is constantly upgrading our revelation and understanding. We need to go deeper than before. Don't be afraid to go deeper and receive greater blessings.

This book is not just theory. I have seen the results of Kim's teaching in her own life and ministry. I have seen her break through into new realms and blessings by doing what she is teaching. You will read her personal testimonies of victory and be encouraged to do the same.

There are practical strategies in this book that churches and individuals can embrace to see greater breakthrough. The revelation in this book will add to a believer's arsenal and help rout the enemy. The watches of the Lord are being restored. Intercessors are taking their place in the church. Apostolic houses of prayer are being established around the globe. Now is the time for the church to arise with a fresh breath and new determination to see the kingdom established.

This book will give not only information but also impartation. As I read the manuscript, I felt a greater anointing and faith for prayer and warfare. The teaching on angels challenged me to be more aware of the conflict that is raging in the heavens. You will be stretched and challenged to do more exploits for the King as you read this book. Personal and corporate victories will come to those who implement these strategies.

I challenge leaders to teach these principles to their congregations. God is calling the assemblies to a greater level of warfare and breakthrough. The cities and regions where we assemble need us to fulfill our calling as believers. Our territories will be blessed if we walk in greater revelation. Revelation is the key to spiritual authority and breakthrough. Jesus is building His church upon the rock of revelation, and the gates of hell will not prevail against it. (See Matthew 16:18.)

In closing, I pray God's blessing upon this book. I pray that it will go to the ends of the earth. I pray that this book will get into the hands of the right people and be a terror to the works of darkness. I pray a blessing upon everyone who reads and implements the teachings in this book. I pray for a spirit of wisdom and revelation to come upon you as you read and study this material.

—JOHN ECKHARDT
APOSTLE AND OVERSEER
OF CRUSADERS MINISTRIES
CHICAGO, IL

AUTHOR'S NOTE: John Eckhardt is my spiritual father and apostolic covering. My national ministry did not bloom until I submitted to his covering. I also had never seen prophetic ministry on the level that Apostle Eckhardt's teams ministered until I met him. Coming in contact with them, I quickly caught on. Many people have asked me about the prophetic anointing on my life. They asked, "How did you get trained, and who taught you to flow?" The answers to these questions are easy: the gift came from God, but John Eckhardt's ministry ignited new levels of prophetic unction in my life. It put a demand on me to stir up the gift. I have never been the same personally or in ministry since our destinies collided.

I am honored to have his words in the beginning pages of this book. True apostles open realms in the spirit to allow entrance into new truths. I intentionally included only a few warfare payers in this book because my apostle wrote a book, *Prayers That Rout Demons and Bring Breakthrough,* during the same time this book was written. I highly recommend this book to use along with the information you are about to read. You may inquire about this book and other materials by Apostle John Eckhardt by calling 708-922-0983.

The Induction

Swearing In

To *BE INDUCTED* means to be formally installed or put into a position or office. As you read this book, it is my prayer that if you have not been inducted into the army of the Lord, this book will make it happen!

When a person is inducted into the natural military, it is for the purpose of training and service. The information in this book has been produced as a result of my experience in spiritual warfare over the past twenty years. I pray that this book will become a tool that God will use to equip and train you for the service of the Lord. I want it to be your induction manual into spiritual warfare in our twenty-first century. It will help you to learn to fight the enemy God's way!

The Lord has blessed me with the experience of an extensive military background. While in the United States Army, I moved through the ranks at an incredible pace. In four years I was promoted to an E-6, or a staff sergeant. Some people retire at this rank after twenty years of service. I attribute my speedy promotion in the military to the fact that I did what was required of me to be eligible. There were prerequisites for promotion. Even when I was not eligible for promotion, I prepared for when my time came. When I became eligible for a rank, the price had already been paid. Promotion in the military is based on the needs of the system. In other words, when there was a demand for my rank and specialty, the army promoted a certain number of soldiers. I made sure that when my number was called, my records were in order to declare my eligibility.

This book is not deep. It is a basic training manual for those who desire to understand the foundational principles of warfare. Many in the body of Christ want to be promoted in the area of spiritual warfare, but they have not taken the time to prepare themselves. They have not met the specifications of the prerequisites. God is calling a muster alert for those in the household of faith to take a radical position against the wiles of the devil. In the military, when a muster alert is called, no one except the highest-ranking officials know if the alert is for training or real war. The motto of the natural army is to be "combat ready." In other words, every time a training exercise or alert is called, soldiers must be ready to respond as if it is a real war.

God is calling His church to a "real war" mentality. Many Christians haphazardly quote, "The weapons of our warfare are not carnal," but fail to walk in the reality of "real war." As a result, people who love God become weary in well doing and acquire a "rolling with the punches" mentality. They are not prepared to deal with the obstacles of life because they have taken everything as it came. They have no basic or advance training in the things of God to teach them how to confront their enemies in victory. My prayer is that this manual will give you a foundation to be prepared for twenty-first-century warfare.

In their warfare today, the natural army is not using catapults and bows and arrows as weapons. This was all right for warfare in centuries past. But today the army uses nuclear weapons. I agree that there is nothing new under the sun, but new truths are being released to the church for today's warfare. These things have been around all the time, but they are new to us. Do not be afraid of what is new to you. Allow the revelations of this book to put a demand on your spirit to go to the next level. You cannot continue to use weapons of times past against twenty-first-century darkness.

The information in this book may seem too radical to you if you are in a comfort zone. If this is the case, I prophesy you out of your comfort zone by the Spirit of the Most High God. I challenge you to plunge into the deeper things of God. I realize that not everyone is called to be a frontline soldier, but I dare you to do the basics that are required of all born-again believers. Mark 16:17–18 (KJV) is our basic training guideline for every believer. The scripture reads:

> And these signs shall follow them that believe; In my name shall they cast out devils; they shall speak with new tongues; they shall take up serpents; and if they drink any deadly thing, it shall not hurt them; they shall lay hands on the sick, and they shall recover.

Always remember that Mark 16:17–18 gives basic foundational instruction for *the everyday believer*!

This passage says that believers must recover. In the Greek, the word *recover* in this passage of Scripture is *ana nephoh,* which means, "to become sober again, to regain one's senses, to recover self." How many people of God have taken arrows from the enemy and have never recovered? David received his marching orders from the Lord and recovered all!

Timothy asked, "How can a bishop take care of the church if he does not have rule in his own home?" (See 1 Timothy 3:5.) This brings one question to my mind. How can we, as the church, win the world if we have no rule in the house of God? I believe this book is a key to releasing the power of God in our own homes and in the church. The key to praying for our churches, communities, and cities is allowing the untapped power of God to flow fluently through us as everyday believers.

The revelations in this book are not limited to those called to the office of the intercessor. If you have been blood bought and are tired of the devil having his way in your affairs, God wants to sign you up for His special forces! When we accept Jesus into our lives, we are automatically signed up for the army of the Lord. Many do not realize it, but they are in the army of the Lord whether they accept it or not. We are not just *members* in the church, but we are *soldiers* for the Lord. Every born-again believer is called to do warfare.

God is taking us past "the right hand of fellowship" (Gal. 2:9), and He is teaching our hands to do war! I want to touch your spirit and agree with you that God would flood your heart with revelation through the contents of this book. By this flood you will have a better understanding of the hope of your calling. Remember, though we walk in the flesh, our warfare is not after the flesh.

After I signed up with the military, there was a grace period before I actually began active duty. Many people make commitments to God but never show up for active duty. The benefits that are afforded to a soldier cannot be received until he or she receives active duty military status. What is your status as God's soldier? Have you sworn in but failed to become *active* in the things of God? Allow the content of this book to activate you, so that in the end you will not stand before the Chief Commander of Creation with your work left undone.

Pray this prayer of agreement with me:

> *Father God, in the name of Jesus, I bind every whispering spirit and strange voice that is set against my spiritual warfare training. My mind is focused on the assignment to finish this book and get what God wants me to have out of it. I take authority over the spirits of imagery and magnification, and I declare that the eyes of my understanding are opened. Mind binders and blinders are blocked and forever bound.*
>
> *I also bind the spirits of slothfulness, slumber, and demonic inertia from causing me to be sleepy when I am reading this book.*

Every distraction is under my feet, and all spirits of doubt have no open place. It is my purpose to tap into the unadulterated truth of God's Word. I am open to new levels of spiritual warfare in my life. Spirits that would prompt "the fear of the unknown" are locked out of my mind. I am not afraid! New boldness is my portion! My spirit is open to agree with the revelations in this book that bear witness with the Holy Spirit. I renounce all religious and familiar spirits that may have influence on the way I receive.

Holy Spirit, I give You permission to deprogram my thinking about anything that has limited the greater works of Jesus Christ in my life. I commit to walk in the anointing of the End-Time believer. All lies and strongholds that have built walls against the truth in my life are pulled down, in Jesus' name. The scales and veils are removed from my eyes so that my understanding will not be hindered.

Lord, I thank You that the words of this book will sharpen my sword and give weight to my realm of influence in the Spirit. This spiritual influence will affect every area of my life and leave an imprint on everything that I put my hands to the plow to do. This spiritual influence will also anoint my steps whereby my footprints will release a centrifugal force in the earth that will confirm the dominion of Christ in my life. I commit to the truth and believe that in every area of my life I will be made free. This liberty will permeate my loins and reproduce freedom in the lives of others. I sign up to be activated for the army of the Lord!

CHAPTER ONE

The Mission

Possessing the Keys

N OW THAT YOU have signed up, you must understand the foundation of the mission. The heartbeat of God is to extend total release to those who have been under the locks and chains of the enemy. The Word of the Lord states that the anointing comes upon us to do several things:

> To preach good tidings to the poor…
> To heal the brokenhearted,
> To proclaim liberty to the captives,
> And the opening of the prison to those who are bound.
> —ISAIAH 61:1

As I read this scripture from the Book of Isaiah, in my spirit I hear one word: *bondage. Bondage* means "to be bound by harness or to have a tight hold of." To *harness* means "to control by the use of power," and *hold* means "to possess by legal right or title or to occupy." Jesus explained the process of bondage to His disciples—and us—in the Gospel of Matthew:

> When an unclean spirit goes out of a man, he goes through dry places, seeking rest, and finds none. Then he says, "I will return to *my house* from which I came." And when he comes, he finds it empty, swept, and put in order. Then he goes and takes with him seven other spirits more wicked than himself, and they enter and dwell there; and the last state of that man is worse than the first. So shall it also be with this wicked generation.
>
> —MATTHEW 12:43–45, EMPHASIS ADDED

The unclean spirit in this scripture refers to the person as "my house." Satan considers us as his belonging (his possession). *My* is defined as "belonging to or in possession of." To have *possession* means "to occupy by driving out the occupying tenants and taking their place." God told Adam to "have dominion" (Gen. 1:26), which means to govern over a territory. He also told Moses, Joshua, and Caleb to go and possess the land. (See Deuteronomy 1:8; Joshua 1:1–11.) Can I be safe in saying that the root of spiritual warfare is *possession*?

Throughout history, the countries that took possession and occupied have been the major world powers. I would like to make a very strong statement that may ruffle some religious feathers, but I'd rather ruffle religious feathers than for God to ruffle mine. *Satan's ultimate goal is to possess!* He does not just want to borrow our souls. He is a wicked tyrant and a hard taskmaster. He lusts for total control. The devil wants to do more than demonize you. He wants total control of your body. He is a wicked body snatcher. In your quest to obey God as a prayer warrior, do not become a casualty or a prisoner of war. Get free and stay free, because your warfare will only go as far as your liberty.

> Do you not know that if you continually surrender yourselves
> to anyone to do his will, you are the slaves of him whom you
> obey?
>
> —ROMANS 6:16, AMP

A slave is a possession. Slaves make no decisions for themselves.
They only do what their master bids them to do.

I have a word of caution for you in warfare prayer: When doing
warfare, do not give demons *a break* or *a rest* by choosing nice words
to avoid offending those who do not understand. Do not surrender
yourself to the devil to do his will. The things we try to avoid, cover
up, or make nice in the church can actually put us in bondage to
the enemy.

The word *bondage* in the Bible is referred to as a yoke. The enemy
controls the yoke. Satan is holding the reins of the yoke. The only
way to deal with a yoke is by utter destruction. The kingdom of God
suffers violence (Matt. 11:12). *Violence* in the Greek is *biazo,* which
means, "seized by force." Many times circumstances and situations
force us into levels of warfare that we never could have imagined
being involved in. This force actually works on our behalf, because it
catapults us into new realms of authority. This authority causes us to
make a transition from being *the seized* to becoming *the seizer.* When
we seize, we take possession of things by legal authority.

The Bible declares that when we recognize a thief, he has to
return sevenfold what was taken. (See Proverbs 6:31.) This means
that because of the assaults that the enemy has launched against us,
we become qualified to walk in new legal authority. The devil has to
pay restitution, and we get what he has stolen back in divine victory.
When we take by force, we get a sevenfold return. On the other hand,
if we sit back and allow the evil to trespass in our lives, it becomes
seven times worse.

Matthew 12:45 speaks of a "wicked generation." This wicked generation is the generation of the demon possessed. These are people
who have been through vicious cycles over and over again. This passage

warns us that if we get delivered and allow demons into our lives again, the bondage will be seven times worse. I often call this spiritual principle "seven and seven." We can take back what the enemy has stolen and receive it back sevenfold, or we can be passive and become seven times worse. In the Greek, the word *wicked* is *poneros*, which is closely related to the word *poneria* ("Spiritual wickedness in high places"— Eph. 6:12, KJV). *Poneros* means "being totally under the influence of the devil." The Greek interpretation shows that the state of this wicked generation is rooted in degeneration. This generation is described as vicious and diseased. Their state is contagious, and they release venom that affects everyone with whom they come in contact.

Why am I explaining the principles of spiritual degeneration? Degeneration has to start from a positive or safe place. People who were never generated cannot degenerate. Degeneration can easily occur when a person attempts to plunge into the deeper things of God with no root in himself or herself. Leaders who have been powerfully used by God are falling by the wayside. We must understand that unto whom much is given, much more is required (Luke 12:48)! Revelation, power, and authority in the Spirit are good things. But on the other hand, without a disciplined lifestyle and a commitment to holiness, these things can be a snare to one's soul.

The strength of any military unit is in the discipline of its soldiers. We strive to obey God, but the precursor to obedience is a disciplined spirit. The only way we can have a disciplined spirit is to be a disciple who is subject to the things of the Spirit. You are a part of a royal priesthood! To sell out to God in intercession and warfare, you must be willing to live a life of the priesthood. The priesthood of which I am speaking of is not one of front rows, nice cars, popularity, and fame. This priesthood is one of persecution, rejection, and separation. These cannot be overcome without spiritual discipline. As soldiers in the army of the Lord, we must learn how to build in the Spirit.

Before anything is built, we must first sit down and count the cost. Jesus warns us in Luke 14:28 that we must first acknowledge our sufficiency to finish. This means that we must know that we have what it takes to finish. If we do not have this security, the Bible says that men will mock what we started because we did not finish (Luke 14:30). Many boldly started out in spiritual warfare, yet their ministries became a mockery. They did not have what it took to finish. This book will equip you to finish! The curse of "not enough" and "almost" will not rule over your head. You will finish because you have been given the keys—use them to bring heaven down to earth!

STEWARDSHIP OF THE KEYS

> And I also say to you that you are Peter, and on this rock I will build My church, and the gates of Hades shall not prevail against it. And I will give you the keys of the kingdom of heaven, and whatever you bind on earth will be bound in heaven, and whatever you loose on earth will be loosed in heaven.
>
> —MATTHEW 16:18–19

The Greek word for *keys* is *klice*, and it is defined as that which locks and unlocks. The keys that Jesus speaks of in Revelation 1:18 and Matthew 16:19 have the same connotation. Based on this, we can be safe in saying that we have been given the power to lock and unlock things in the earth. These keys must be used with wisdom and anointing. Some Christians have used their keys in ignorance and are living under a locked (closed) heaven. On the other hand, some have not put their keys to use at all. A key that is never used is of no effect. Keys represent the ability to enter and have authority! A person who does not know how to use the keys that Jesus has given him has no authority and has no ability to enter into what God has for him.

When keys are used, they must be strategically put in place. Even when using a key in the natural, there is a way to insert it in the lock. If someone attempts to put a key in a keyhole sideways or upside down it will not fit. Just so, we must have the strategies of the Holy Ghost to use the keys that Jesus has given us. Along with strategy, we need maturity and wisdom. Can you imagine a five-year-old sitting in the front seat of a car with the keys to drive it? That child is not mature enough to drive a car.

This is the case with some believers. Because they have been kept on milk, they are like babies with keys to a car when it comes to spiritual warfare. This is why it is important that at some time people be taken off of what Paul called "spiritual milk" (1 Cor. 3:2). Milk is great for children up to a certain age, but after children begin to get teeth, they need to have meat. The information in this book has been written in maturity and wisdom to enable believers to come off of the milk and cut their teeth on solid principles of warfare prayer. My vision is to teach the masses how to embark upon spiritual warfare and finish in victory with the booty. When the people of God won battles in the Bible, they came out with the spoils of their enemies. When you bind the strongman, YOU GET THE GOODS!

The Bible clearly states that there is a way that seems right to a man, but the end of it is death (Prov. 14:12). It is a deadly endeavor to ignorantly use the keys that Jesus gave. God said, "My people are destroyed for lack of knowledge" (Hos. 4:6). The spiritual system of binding and loosing must operate in accordance with the plan of God to produce its full potential. To *bind* is *deo* or *deomai* in the Greek. This means to create a knot through prayer that is impossible to uncoil. The word *loose* in the Greek is *luo*, and means to break the barrier or to lacerate (to make an opening). Spiritual loosing does not only consist of a "sending forth"; it also entails tearing down the strongholds that Satan puts between our promise and us. After we have bound demonic operation, we must release the promise. *Luo* means to cause a release that gives room to a breaking forth.

For our purposes, we will take note of three different definitions for the word *keys*:

1. "To have access": A *place* that is located in a position as to give control of a region (example: Key West, Florida).

2. "To know": A *thought* that brings revelation and solves answers to questions.

3. "To control": A *thing* that physically lets one in or locks one out.

All of the above have one root word in common: *authority*. The sole desire of the enemy is to *have access*, to *know*, and to *control*, but God has given that authority to us. We have what it takes, so the devil wants what we have. He does not have the ability to finish, because he automatically loses in the end. So you see, these keys are special; they give us power over darkness. If we do not use them, we will lose them!

When it comes to spiritual warfare, we have been losing ground in the Spirit for too long because of ignorance. We must get in place to stand against the wiles of darkness in the last days. How can we stand against the wiles of the enemy when we are ignorant of his devices? The Bible declares that we should not be ignorant of the devices of the evil one (2 Cor. 2:11). So, if we have been ignorant, we have been in sin!

To become aware of the devices of Satan is a special type of liberty. It is the liberty that Paul experienced when he said that he was not just swinging at air but he had a specific enemy (1 Cor. 9:26). Isn't it great to know that you have not been tripping? You have not lost your mind, because the spirit realm is as much a reality as the natural realm.

The Word of the Lord pronounces that unto whom much is given, much is required (Luke 12:48). We are living in a day when everyone wants authority. Everyone wants to be in charge! When God delegates authority, there is a strict accountability. The first thing an ambassador of the Lord must do in this authority is to separate from anything that would coincide with darkness. We are warned in the Word not to conform to the world. The prefix *con-* means to work with or come into agreement with. We cannot come up against Satan and be in agreement with him at the same time.

God commands us to "give no room (access) to the enemy." (See Ephesians 4:27.) How do we give room to the enemy? One of the greatest ways to give room to the enemy is by neglecting to use the authority that God has given us "to stand in the gap" (Ezek. 22:30). If we do not stand in the gap for our coast, demons will displace us and control our destinies.

CHAPTER TWO

Demonic Transmissions

Satan's Communication System

A N ARMY WITHOUT effective communication will be defeated. Any antagonistic force against an army will attempt to infiltrate that army's communication system. The devil attempts to block our communication with our Holy Ghost headquarters by way of spiritual attacks through mental captivation. When a person's mind is captivated, it has been charmed by seducing spirits and kidnapped. Ultimately, the attention of that person is rerouted.

Captivation is the hijacking of the mind in a deceptive manner. Because the mind has the ability to send transmissions to the body to tell it what to do, the enemy infiltrates it. His goal is to have free course in the body. To break free of the devil's captivation, the powers of demonic transmission must be broken. When this occurs, the connection of the mind to his control is severed.

How does the devil communicate with us? Let's look at the transmissions of the demonic communication cycle.

SATAN'S COMMUNICATION CYCLE

SENDER
Devil

1. IDEA
—Imagination
—Plot of the
  enemy

2. ENCODING
The enemy makes
the message
receivable (tailor-
made for you).
—Right words
—Supportive
  materials
—Pitch of voice

3. TRANSMISSION
The medium or
channeler the enemy
uses to send the
message can be a
person, place, or
thing. He will use
whoever or whatever
is:
—Available
—Reachable
—Accessible

7. FEEDBACK
The only thing you should
send back is the Word. Make
the devil take it back!

Positive feedback or response
improves or gives power to
what was sent.

Negative feedback breaks the
communication cycle!

RECEIVER
You

6. UNDERSTANDING
You cannot come into
agreement with what the devil
is sending in your mind.
Have this attitude!
—I do not receive this.
—I cannot see this.

5. DECODING
—Break it down
—Discerning
—What does this
  mean?
—Who did it
  come from?
—Interpretation
  of what is really
  going on

4. RECEIVING
Getting the attention
of; exposure, making
known

This illustration of the communication cycle serves two purposes:

1. It helps believers to understand how to reject demonic thoughts at the inception of the attack against the mind.

2. It provides a strategy for sending all negativity and curses that have matured in the lives of believers back to their point of origination.

You must understand that when the enemy sends negative thoughts your way, it is a literal attack against your mind. You cannot downplay these attacks and make them less important than they are.

The first step to liberation from these communication tactics is developing the ability to recognize thoughts that are not of God. You must identify these thoughts and send them back immediately. They must not be encoded into your mind. Do not give the enemy room! Do not try to discern or figure out crazy thought patterns that the devil sends to your mind. Do not entertain foreign thoughts! Cast down every evil imagination upon its inception, and there will be no demonic transmissions into your life.

Remember that there is a difference between your *mind* and your *thoughts*. Your mind is the vehicle, and your thoughts are what you allow to get into your vehicle and ride. Do not pick up strangers to ride in the vehicle of your mind! You do not have to be delivered from what you will cast down first.

In other words, in spiritual warfare we are casting out of people what they should have cast down in the first place. The enemy wants to use our minds as his battlefield, and he will continue to launch attacks. No matter what anybody tells you, the devil desires to control your soul. He does not just want a ride in your vehicle—he wants to be in the driver's seat of your mind, will, intellect, and emotions.

Demons want to come into our lives and rest! Recently I was ministering deliverance to a young man who was bound by generational witchcraft in his family. The demons began to cry out in him at a Sunday night service. I have heard demons speak through people, but this night it shook my soul. The words that the demon spoke through the young man baffled me, but as I sought the Lord, things became clearer. The demon said, "You have awakened me from my sleep!"

This young man had a beautiful family, but he could not shake his desire to leave his family for the streets. The strongman in his life, which was the spirit of death, had taken up residence in his life to the point that that spirit was comfortable and at rest.

The night before the church service, a spirit that looked like the Grim Reaper had come into the young man's bedroom. The young man testified that the smell of sulfur came into the room. Whenever the smell of sulfur manifests itself in the natural realm, the portals of hell have been opened and have released an assignment. This incident made him run to church.

The day that he arrived at our church was during the week of Passover. I declared "Passover deliverance" over him, and the ministry team prayed for him. The demon that was sleeping in his life was awakened, and we cast him out! If we allow the transmissions of the enemy to enter our thought lives, it will give demons rest.

There are two major components of the communication cycle:

- The sending (transmission)
- The receiving (reception)

In the case of the communication cycle, the devil is the sender, and the human mind is in the position of the receiver. God gave us a will! We have the ability to take authority over the airways of our minds by allowing the Holy Spirit to be the air traffic controller. The devil is a spiritual terrorist, and he is always seeking entrance to the headquarters of the body, which is the mind! The most productive way to deal with terrorism is to block all entry points and destroy the plans of the enemy at inception. This is why we must have the mind of Christ. It is a safeguard against mental terrorism.

Demonic transmission does not take place overnight. It is a process! When the devil sends demonic transmissions against your mind, you must stop his progression at the beginning of the attack. The longer thoughts linger, the more influence they have! When the enemy sends negative thoughts, it is a literal attack against your mind.

The major attack against intercessors is the spirit of distraction. Distractions do not just happen by chance. They are strategic assignments sent to break focus. If the enemy breaks your focus, he can break your flow. Intercessors must have spiritual continuity or the ability to continue without wandering off course. Distractions that attack the mind hinder the ability to move on, and completion never takes place. This creates loose ends!

When a person has too many loose ends in their life, their discernment is eventually blocked. Having keen discernment is the first step in dealing with things that come to distract the mind. Thoughts that are not of God must be identified and sent back immediately. They must not be encoded (received) and decoded (processed) into our minds. Do not give the enemy room! It is futile to attempt to discern the crazy things the devil sends to our minds. Again, I reiterate, do not entertain foreign thoughts! Foreign thoughts are thoughts that do not produce a kingdom mentality. If thoughts do not line up with what the kingdom of heaven says about the situation, reject them!

Remember that your mind is the vehicle, and your thoughts represent what you allow to get into your vehicle. Do not pick up strange hitchhikers to ride in the vehicle of your mind! Remember, you do not have to be delivered from what you cast down first.

TAKING ANOTHER LOOK AT THE COMMUNICATION CYCLE

The chart shown at the beginning of this chapter starts with an idea that must be encoded into our minds to transmit the plan of the enemy. Transmissions are sent by people, places, or things. Note that the enemy will use any person, place, or thing that is accessible or available for him to channel through. Once things are transmitted, they have the opportunity of being received. Once they are received, the enemy has gained access or room!

After reception it is a downhill run for the enemy. When I think of reception, I think about cell phones or radios. If I am in certain parts of town where the towers for phones or radios do not get good reception, I cannot receive phone calls or radio messages. This should be a revelation to us! We need to be in a place in the Spirit where the towers (strongholds) of the enemy have no reception. That which cannot be received cannot be decoded.

To decode a thing has to do with discerning, and this leads to understanding. Prayer warriors must have balance when dealing in spiritual warfare. Though we must be able to recognize the devices of the enemy, we must not entertain them and give the devil more credit than he deserves. As prayer warriors we should not be motivated by what the devil is doing, but only by what God is doing. There are certain things on which the enemy does not even deserve feedback. When the surrounding enemies of the Israelites tried to distract Nehemiah from his task of rebuilding the walls, he told his enemies, "I am not coming down off the wall!" (See Nehemiah 6:3.) Our only response to the transmissions of the enemy must be the Word of God. When Jesus was tempted by the devil in the wilderness, He responded by declaring the Word of God. Notice that the communication cycle of the enemy begins with a simple idea. Every idea of the enemy is a lie fixed up to look like the truth to our minds. Our minds must be renewed by the Word of God to the point that the lies of the enemy will not compute.

Understanding the principle of demonic transmission helps us to understand how to reverse curses and send them back. Curses are transmitted or sent on spiritual waves that have a point of origination and a destination. Many curses will not cease to operate unless they are sent back to the point of their origination or cursed at the roots. In either situation, the curse must be dealt with at its root or entry point. During deliverance sessions people have often received major breakthroughs when the entry points of the demons were revealed.

Jesus cursed the fig tree from its roots.

> Now in the morning, as they passed by, they saw the fig tree dried up from the roots.
>
> —MARK 11:20

Nehemiah reversed the curses that his enemies sent to stop him from rebuilding the walls of Jerusalem. Let's take a look at the scriptures:

> [And Nehemiah prayed] Hear, O our God, for we are despised. Turn their taunts upon their own heads, and give them for a prey in a land of their captivity. Cover not their iniquity and let not their sin be blotted out before You, for they have vexed [with alarm] the builders and provoked You.
>
> —NEHEMIAH 4:4–6, AMP

The Bible does tell us to bless those that come up against us, but in these two instances this was not the case. Jesus cursed the roots of the fig tree, and Nehemiah reversed the curses of his enemies. The Bible says that he "turned" their reproach upon their own heads. The word *turned* in the Hebrew is *shuwb,* and it means to send it back! Many Christians are uncomfortable sending curses back because they are unfamiliar with this biblical concept. In other countries, people pray according to the Word of God. America has become comfortable concerning the things of God. Intellect and education have replaced the apostolic and prophetic ministries that men displayed in the Bible.

This is the strategy of the enemy. He is using the intellect and religious education of which we in America are so proud against us. Please hear me out! I am for education, and I do not believe that God wants us to be ignorant to the things of the natural. My problem is that preachers have allowed intellect to override the things of the Spirit. They have become natural men. It is a curse to be a natural man. Natural men cannot discern the things of the Spirit. The Bible says that spiritual things are foolishness to them because such things can only be spiritually discerned (1 Cor. 2:14). Let's review the scriptures on this:

> [This is] because the foolish thing [that has its source in] God is wiser than men, and the weak thing [that springs] from God is stronger than men.
>
> —I CORINTHIANS 1:25, AMP

Things that are foolish to most people in the church actually have their source in God. Paul was a learned man, so he was not mocking the naturally wise. Paul knew how to abound and to be abased. He was educated by the religious system, and yet he went to the school of the Holy Ghost to receive apostolic revelation.

Paul went on to say that God intentionally chose what was foolish to put the wise to shame (v. 27). He quoted God in Isaiah 29:14 when He said: "I will baffle and render useless and destroy the learning of the learned and the philosophy of the philosophers and the cleverness of the clever and the discernment of the discerning; I will frustrate and nullify [them] and bring [them] to nothing. Where is the wise man (the philosopher)? Where is the scribe (the scholar)? Where is the investigator (the logician, the debater) of this present time and age?" (1 Cor. 1:19–20, AMP).

God was calling the smart folk out, and He did not sound too pleased with them. He does not take it well when men use the abilities that He has given them to take His glory. To know it all in God is to know nothing. When we try to know it all, God will personally bring us down to nothing.

Demonic transmissions flow fluently through intellect without God. It is the number one way that people are deceived, because it breeds unteachable spirits. Romans 8:6 (AMP) refers to this kind of intellect as "the mind of the flesh [which is sense and reasoning without the

Holy Spirit]." The devil is looking for believers who think they know it all. This ungodly mind-set puts people in the place where they are forever learning but never coming to the truth. They have forms of godliness on the outside but resist the true essence of what is really important to God.

Yes, we must send demonic transmissions back, but this is impossible to do without a renewed mind. Our minds are continually renewed by the Word of God. As people of God, we never fully arrive when it comes to renewal. Our minds must be continually renewed with the Word of God to stand against the attacks of the enemy.

REVERSING CURSES

The enemy does not play fair. He always has a strategy. He does not waste his time attacking people who are not doing anything. Nehemiah was not attacked until the walls of Jerusalem started to go up. When Sanballat heard that Nehemiah was building, he launched his attack. (See Nehemiah 4.) He attacked when Nehemiah started acting upon what he had already said. The enemy is not distracted in his battle plan by people who are just talking. Many people talk about their visions but never put their hands to the plow to make their visions manifest.

Nehemiah manifested his vision before devils, and they were mad. When Nehemiah's enemies attacked, they did not shoot natural weapons. *They sent words!* This is the same strategy that the enemy uses today: "word warfare." The old saying "Sticks and stones may break my bones, but words can never hurt me" is not true when it comes to Satan's tactics. People can recover easier from attacks by sticks and stones than from word curses. A word curse in a person's life is like cancer that has gone ignored. By the time a word curse has run its course in a life, it takes the supernatural intervention of God to put an end to it.

This is why we must deal with attacks of demonic word curses at their inception. Nehemiah never heeded the words of his enemies.

His only response was to say that he was not coming down off the wall! This is the ultimate ploy of the enemy; he wants to distract us long enough to cause us to give up. Nehemiah kept his commitment to complete the work of rebuilding the wall. Although his enemies grew in strength and number, the work was never stopped. His determination to reverse the curse Sanballat intended to hurl at him was totally effective.

From this illustration of Nehemiah, we learn that the reverse of a curse is scripturally orchestrated when two things happen. (See Nehemiah 4:4–5.)

1. Curses are sent to stop the work of God.

2. God Himself is provoked, and He uses an individual under apostolic mandate to release His righteous judgment.

The demonic transmissions of the enemy never took root in Nehemiah's mind. He achieved this victory from his defensive position. But Nehemiah did not stop there—he got on the offense. He prayed a prayer to reverse the things that his enemies had sent to linger over his head. He reversed the curse!

> [And Nehemiah prayed] Hear, O our God, for we are despised. Turn their taunts upon their own heads, and give them for a prey in a land of their captivity. Cover not their iniquity and let not their sin be blotted out before You, for they have vexed [with alarm] the builders and provoked You.
>
> —Nehemiah 4:4–5, amp

Vexation is a type of witchcraft. Through manipulation it disturbs a person's peace. It rides the nerves of a person and annoys them until they are affected in their minds. The builders were under attack in their minds, and Nehemiah sent the curse back. Sometimes curses must be broken corporately because they have been sent against an entire house. The enemy especially likes to vex the minds of those who build in the church. Many are building churches, but they do not know how to *build in the church*. There is a difference. When we build in the church it edifies the body and equips the saints.

I prophesy that those who build in the church will not be vexed to the point of coming off the wall. The church is doing a great work, and we will not be distracted by the voices of our enemies.

CHAPTER THREE

Putting Your Finger on the Enemy

*Identify, Expose, and
Incapacitate the Strongman*

THE BIBLE COMMANDS us to stand against the wiles of the enemy (Eph. 6:11). The wiles of the enemy are the ways in which the devil conducts his business. Mark 3:27 says, "No one can enter a strongman's house and plunder his goods, unless he first binds the strongman. And then he will plunder his house."

How can you bind what you do not know exists? In doing warfare and deliverance over the past twenty years, I have found that the more I put my finger on the devil, the less effective he is. Satan's power only operates by imagery and magnification.

By identifying him and exposing his work, it causes him, and his kingdom, to be incapacitated. This can be illustrated by observing how terrorism can be stopped when nations are able to identify terrorists and their wicked plots. If the United States had more secret intelligence on terrorists, our ability to war against our unseen enemies would be greatly enhanced.

It is unwise for believers to say that they do not need to know about the devil. It is because the church has tiptoed through the tulips in this area that we have become ignorant of the devices of the enemy. As a result of our lack of knowledge about our enemy, we often find ourselves warring against each other because we cannot discern who our real enemy is. This activity can be identified as *friendly fire.* In the natural military, friendly fire is what happens when forces on the same team take each other out. People who do not have the ability to recognize their enemy tend to shoot ammunition at friendly forces or innocent bystanders. The terrible thing is that while they are targeting friendly forces, their real foes go unnoticed. This is why Jude 4 speaks of the enemy creeping in the church unnoticed.

Jesus knew who His enemies were! He identified them, even among His own followers! Demons are hiding out in our churches today. In the Bible, when Jesus or the spotlight of His Word came on the scene, the devils came out of hiding. They manifested!

This brings an important question to my mind: Is Jesus really "on the scene" in some of today's churches?

JESUS' MODEL FOR DEALING WITH SPIRITS

We should deal with spirits the way Jesus dealt with them. When Jesus confronted demons, He was very specific about what He was dealing with.

- *Jesus identified spirits.* He identified the foul spirit as a deaf and dumb spirit (Mark 9:25).

- *Jesus asked the spirits to identify themselves.* He asked the demons in the demoniac, "What is your name?" The demon replied, "My name is Legion; for we are many" (Mark 5:9).

- *Jesus made a clear distinction that all demons were not the same.* He stated, "This kind does not go out except by prayer and fasting" (Matt. 17:21).

- *Jesus referred to Beelzebub as the prince of the devils.* This proves that Beelzebub was not just a regular spirit. He had a special position and assignment (Matt. 12:24).

Satan's power is dependent upon deception and secrecy. As long as he can operate behind the scenes, he can strengthen his operation and make his target weaker. The word *occult* means "in secret" or "in darkness." When it comes to spiritual warfare, an uninformed church is a target for the enemy to attack at will.

Many churches believe that they do not have to do deliverance and warfare because they never see manifestations of the devil. This is a very dangerous thing to believe! Is it that these ministries have no manifestations because they are free of demonic activity, or is it because devils are hiding in their pulpits and pews? Devils manifested in the synagogues that Jesus visited, and I would be afraid if they did not manifest in mine. We cannot cast out what does not manifest, and that which is never cast out remains!

Pastors have come to me to tell me that demons were starting to manifest in their churches. This is a *good thing*! It means that the devils that have been there all the time are coming out of hiding and can be dealt with. Many believers who do not have the ability to put their finger on the enemy live a tormenting life of guerrilla warfare. They are continually under attack by an enemy that they cannot see. Some preachers are dying early. Infirmity is running rampant in the church, and our children are bound.

The highest level of guerrilla warfare is to fight an enemy on his own turf. As a young girl, I grew up fighting in the streets of Jacksonville, Florida. I was a strategic fighter. I knew who to fight, when to fight, when to make friends, and when to run. This helped me to have a good winning record. I did not lose many fights, and it was not because I could not be beaten. To survive on the streets you have to have more than a good right-hand punch; you must be able to out-think your enemies. The best way for me to get the upper hand on a person in a fight was to get that person in my own yard. If I was going to be beaten, it would not be in my own yard. Everyone knows that in a football game the home team has the advantage.

The devil is the god of this world and the prince of the power of the air. But God has given us dominion to walk in the authority that Jesus Christ gave back to us on Calvary. That dominion gives us home court advantage. Yet many preach about Calvary but fail to walk in the power of Calvary. The real power of what happened on the cross is the fact that Jesus disarmed principalities and "made a public spectacle of them" (Col. 2:15)! He busted the devil out then, and we should purpose to continue to bust him out today. When we cast out devils and do spiritual warfare, we bring to fruition the finished work of the cross. In that process we take back from Satan all the things he has stolen from us.

The ministry of casting out devils is the highest level of spiritual warfare. It is ground-level warfare, and the Bible says that when we do it, THE KINGDOM HAS COME (Matt. 12:28)! I get stirred in my soul when I think about it. I do not want to spend my walk with God walking under a gray cloud. I do not have to walk around sensing that something is wrong in my life and never be able to put my finger on what it is. Do you feel as though shadows are following you around? Do you feel as if you are walking under a dark cloud? I have a revelation for you—what you are feeling is just as real as what you cannot see!

The terror in guerrilla warfare is that you cannot put your finger on your enemy. He is everywhere and could be anywhere. For the believer engaged in spiritual guerrilla warfare, our enemy is the prince of the power of the air! How do we put our finger on air? We do it through spiritual warfare!

We cannot pray everyday prayers when the hordes of hell are after our children. We cannot depend on natural resources when we are under spiritual attack. This is why so many Christians are going to psychologists and are addicted to prescription drugs. They cannot put their finger on their enemy. God is calling us to put our fingers on the enemy and squash him. When we begin to recognize the devil for who he really is, we will see that he is like an ant in a cage with an elephant when it comes to the kingdom of God. He is so small and insignificant when we can put our finger on him. But when he goes unnoticed and overlooked, he seems to become a giant in our land.

When all is said and done, many who have been deceived by the enemy will say, "Is this that man?" The Bible says he has made kingdoms fall and great men tumble. One day, in the eyes of those he has deceived, he will be pinned on the walls of the pit with a safety pin. When they see the devil for how small he really is, they will be ashamed to know that the prince of the power of the air was a joke. That's right, the devil is a joke to those who know how to put their finger on him.

Warfare is walking in victory over the spirit of magnification. This is a world-ruling spirit that makes the satanic kingdom appear bigger than what it really is. Spiritual warfare removes this magnifying glass and reveals darkness for what it really is—an illusion of victory. When I am under great attack, my mind-set is, "It isn't real!" The Word of God is more real to me than the attacks of the devil. If my healing is real, then sickness is a delusion. I do not ignore attacks, but this confession has saved my life many times.

THE DEMONIC HIERARCHY OF THE ENEMY

When Jesus walked the earth, He had a revelation of the spirit realm (good and evil). The more that light is shed on the dark areas of Satan's operation, the less effective he is. We understand that Satan is our ultimate enemy, but we must come to the realization that he has cohorts that work for him. There is a well-organized demonic kingdom.

One of the ranks of the demonic order is the *kosmokrator* or world ruler. The sixth chapter of Ephesians speaks of the rulers of the darkness of this world (v. 12). The kosmokrator controls the order of the cosmos or the world order. In my book *Clean House, Strong House*, I teach on this in depth.[1] There is a need to understand the levels of devils and their specific operations.

A strongman is a ground-level devil that guards and controls the traffic of strongholds. Strongholds form keys in the spirit that lock demons into the lives of people so that they cannot be free. The demons that we cast out of people are disembodied spirits. They require a body to express themselves in the natural realm. In this chapter I will address the powers of the air and deal with the satanic rank of the demonic kingdom.

The strategy to pull down demonic strongholds of the enemy is focused upon paying attention to detail. The enemy's kingdom must be broken up in parts and dealt with accordingly. This is a foundational principle of territorial warfare. In the pages that follow, I will list the hierarchy of the satanic kingdom. I believe that this is the order of the kingdom of darkness. Principalities, powers, ruler spirits, and spiritual wickedness in high places are the powers of the air. Satan is the prince of the powers of the air.

The word *air* refers to vicious cycles. These demons oversee the strongholds of cycles and recurring curses. This is why ground-level warfare cannot be successful unless the powers of the air are dealt with. The powers of the air are also known as fallen angels, because they were cast out of heaven with Lucifer. Thank God that only one-third of the angels fell from heaven with the devil. There are more for us than can ever be against us.

WHAT IS THE ORDER
OF THE SATANIC KINGDOM?

Satanic hierarchy (and their assignment)

Satan—the prince of the power of the air

Beelzebub—the prince of the devils (see special comment on next page), answers directly and only to Satan

Principalities—princes of the four corners of the earth (continents, countries, states, cities, counties), arch magistrates or principal demons; first in rank

Powers—organizations (*exousia*—special ability, highly competent; liberty In jurisdiction)

Ruler spirits—neighborhoods, families, individuals (*kosmokrator*—world ruler, spirits with direct contact with their targets)

Spiritual wickedness in high places—idolatry (Hezekiah tore down the high places) (*poneria*—iniquity and malice, sin and idolatrous activity

SPECIAL COMMENT: Princes of devils are assigned by era. During Jesus' life, Beelzebub was the prince of the devils. During Elijah's life, Baal was the prince of the ruling force of devils. It has also been noted that Dagon was the prince of devils during another era.

To be effective against any enemy in warfare, you must know as much about that enemy as possible. It is understood that Satan is the archenemy of God, but he does not work alone. We have many enemies, because there are many devils. In the dark kingdom there is an unimaginable dedicated order. Demons walk in this order with uncompromising commitment to the devil. They fear breaking rank, and every position gets the respect that it is due.

> For we do not wrestle against flesh and blood but against *principalities*, against *powers*, against the *rulers of the darkness* of this world, against *spiritual wickedness in high places*.
> —EPHESIANS 6:12, KJV, EMPHASIS ADDED

Looking at the list in this verse, let's walk through each rank.

Principalities

The Greek word for *principalities* is *arche,* and it is related to the English word *arch*, which means to be chief. Principalities are chief devils. The Greek word *arche* means to be first in time, rank, or order. It also means to have first rule.

The Bible states that God also has an order for the church. First Corinthians 12:28 says that God has set some in the church: "first apostles, secondarily prophets, thirdly teachers" (KJV). The word *first* in this scripture is *proton*, and it means "first in order of importance." Why would God say that apostles are first in order of importance? I believe that it is because apostles are specifically assigned to go into regions and set their faces against principalities. God has set the first (*arche*) against the first (*proton*). This does not mean that only apostles can deal with principalities. It only means that they are specifically set aside to do it.

Powers

The word *powers* in the Greek is *exousia*. As I mention in the chapter on witchcraft, power spirits are specialists. They are the FBI and CIA of the demonic rank. When other spirits cannot get the job done, Satan dispatches power spirits against God's people. If you would like to know more about power spirits, see the chapter in this book on witchcraft.

The rulers of the darkness of this world

Ruler spirits are the demons of the cosmos or world rulers. The word *ruler* in the Greek is *kosmokrator,* and it means "world ruler." In 2 Corinthians 4:4, the Bible says that if the gospel is hidden, it is hidden by the god of this world. The kosmokrator hides the truth and blinds the minds of people through cosmetic deception. Ruler spirits rule over regions and make fetishes look like fads and witchcraft look like family traditions. They make murder look like a life choice and homosexuality look like a lifestyle. These demons are experts at making people worship the devil without knowing it. To break peer pressure off of our children, we must dismantle the power of world rulers from over their heads.

Spiritual wickedness in high places

Spiritual wickedness in high places is demonic influence from the second heaven, which makes things worse in the world. The word *wickedness* is *poneros* in the Greek, and it means "to cause degeneration." Let's look at Matthew 12:45:

> Then he goes and takes with him seven other spirits more wicked than himself, and they enter and dwell there; and the last state of that man is worse than the first. So shall it also be with this wicked generation.

The word *wicked* is the same in Ephesians 6:12 and Matthew 12:45. They both mean "to degenerate or to become worse in state." Spiritual wickedness in high places influences those who have influence in the earth. These demonic assignments infiltrate governmental entities, denominational headquarters, Hollywood, professional athletics, and much more. The key word is *influence*. Wherever influence abides, power and money will not be far away.

These demonic deities are territorial in nature as they operate by specific assignment. Their goal is to infiltrate and degenerate. The homosexual agenda operates fluently under this principle. The homosexual agenda is a long-term strategy. The heads of this agenda are very patient. They have worked to set representatives in high places of influence throughout the land. They head educational, judicial, penal, financial, corporate, entertainment, and religious systems, and they use their places of influence to promote their twisted views. Because of their status, the general population can easily become more compassionate toward their campaign and more willing to receive it as normal.

These world leaders ultimately use their high places of authority to infiltrate others like them to secure their realm of influence. This is why the attitude toward the homosexual agenda has become more user friendly in America. As an illustration, one school board super-intendent of a major city listed his live-in mate (another man) in his inaugural program. He boldly and publicly announced in writing that he was living with a man. This same superintendent has fired many godly principals in the area and hired homosexuals to replace them. The root of this entire assignment is seated in the second heaven. It can be overturned if the saints will petition the higher court in the third heaven.

GROUND-LEVEL DEVILS

The demons that we cast out of people are not a part of the satanic hierarchy that I have just listed. When we do warfare against the satanic hierarchy, these spirits must be pulled down. Ground-level devils or disembodied spirits must be cast out! These devils must have a body to express themselves. When they are cast out, they are sent into places of torment and punishment. This is why the demons asked Jesus' permission to go into the pigs. They need a host to rest in.

Powers of the air rule from their positions in the second heaven. Using demonic cords, they have connections to people in the earth, who become like spiritual puppets on strings. Ephesians 2:2 speaks of how the prince of the power of the air rules over the children of disobedience. These people are noted as being careless, rebellious, and unbelieving. They are connected to the second heaven, just as people are seated in heavenly places with Christ Jesus. Every human being is connected to the second or third heaven spiritually. At times, people must first be disconnected from second heaven activity in order to receive full deliverance.

We will take a closer look at the ground-level devils.

Satan's imps

Satan has hordes of helpers, but I would like to bring attention to a few. These demonic imps are so dumb that they do not think for themselves. They only have the ability to follow orders. They have small detailed assignments to which they are highly dedicated.

Watchers

These are demons that are set up like surveillance cameras. They attach themselves to stationary objects for one reason only—to provide surveillance. These spirits operate as third eyes to focus in on their assignment. The satanic headquarters can view activity through these watchers. They never move unless they are cast out of a place or their assignment is over.

Scanners

These are demons that can scan things, as a copy machine scans, and then take the pictures back to the satanic headquarters. They take snapshots of incidents to use as evidence against the brethren. Satan is the accuser of the brethren, and he gathers evidence for his cases against the saints.

Eavesdroppers

These demons are like demonic tape recorders. Conversations are recorded and taken back to the satanic headquarters to keep on record until they need to be used against a saint.

The devil is not omnipotent, omnipresent, or omniscient. He cannot be in all places at once (as God can), he does not know everything (as God does), and he does not have all power (as God does). Because of this, he has demons that work for him to assist him where he is limited. There is a realm in the spirit where *akashic records* are filed. When we are forgiven by God, He throws all of our faults into the sea of forgetfulness. On the other hand, the devil attempts to pull them up and hold them over our heads. The records of these things are kept in a place in the spirit called the *akashic records*. Psychics and people who operate through third eyes pull their information from this place. They cannot tap into the power of God, so they use this demonic source.

For example, a psychic can demonically tap into these files and give a person accurate information pertaining to their circumstances. I found out about the akashic records as I was praying for witches that wanted to renounce Satan and serve the Lord. There is literature on this realm, but I do not recommend researching it out. Without the unction of the Holy Ghost, digging into information like this can open doors in the spirit that do not need to be opened. The important thing we need to know is that there is a realm where this does exist. To bind demonic activity that relates to slander, faultfinding, accusation, lies, defamation of character, and demonic reproach, we can come against the work of the place where the akashic files are kept.

CHAPTER FOUR

Witchcraft and Divination

Witchcraft

WITCHCRAFT IS THE practice, power, and use of the supernatural without the intervention of the Holy Spirit. It cannot be argued that anyone who operates in this power knowingly or unknowingly is a witch. There are only two powers that exist. They are the power of God and the power of the devil. The power of the devil is simply witchcraft!

Many will deny that there is a thin line between darkness and light. But this line is so thin that many on God's side unknowingly slip to the other side and become witches. A *witch* is defined as a person who works witchcraft.

I would like to discuss three categories of witches:

1. Blind (or natural) witches

These are people who have been dedicated to be witches but have no awareness of it. I call these people "empty shells." They are ignorantly used by witchcraft powers. Most blind witches are aware that they have special power, but they are deceived as to its real source. Some cases are so extreme that it seems that demons have knocked the victims out and are living through their lives. These people do not go out of their way to operate in the supernatural; they are simply "natural witches."

Often I have heard people say that they were born with a veil over their face, or that they have been known to have *special* powers. The ironic thing is that they have no relationship with Christ! This is demonic and should be renounced. I know that babies have no control over their birth situation. On the other hand, to agree with the superstitious belief of the veiled face opens the door to demonic dedication. All power outside of Christ must be renounced and put under the blood of Jesus.

Many people have told me that they do not understand why, but they "just know things." This means that a third eye must be closed in their foreheads. Psychics operate through third eyes and the manipulation of the spirit realm.

The greatest spiritual principle to understand in dealing with the supernatural is this: everything that God has, the devil has a counterfeit for it! For instance, let's take a look at the Greek word for *power, exousia.*

> Behold, I give unto you power to tread on serpents and scorpions, and over all the power of the enemy.
>
> —LUKE 10:19, KJV

This scripture describes the dominion God has given us over dark powers. When this passage refers to "the power to tread on serpents," it is addressing *exousia* power. On the other hand, when it refers to having power "over all the power of the enemy," it is declaring *dunamis*, or miracle-working power. *Exousia* is the power of a potentate or specialist. It is defined as special ability and competency to master a designated jurisdiction. Though we are all in the forces of the Lord, a person with *exousia* is like the CIA or FBI of the force. Many witches who come to the Lord continue to struggle with their salvation because they never renounce their "power spirits" or demonic *exousia*. These "power spirits" give them supernatural ability to manipulate the spirit realm to affect natural circumstances and situations. This is an example of demonic *exousia*.

2. Functional witches

Functional witches are witches who operate in a demonic premeditation. In other words, they have carefully thought-out plans for working darkness against innocent bystanders. They function as everyday people and operate incognito. They are outright enemies who plant themselves in our midst and take pride in their secret plans.

Jude 4 speaks of how men creep into the midst of God's people and remain there "unawares." The Greek word for *unawares* is *pareisduno,* and it means "to settle in alongside." Witches have been settling in our churches without being detected since the church started. An example of a functional witch in the Bible is the woman with the spirit of divination who followed the disciples around many days. She pretended to be for them until it was discovered who she really was (Acts 16:16). This spirit was cast out through discernment.

Many believers have discernment, but they ignore the warnings of the Holy Spirit for one reason or the other. To most Christians, it is hard to believe that there are people from the other side who would take the time to establish themselves in our midst. I have a very good friend who has a large ministry. He understood the supernatural, but he could not fathom enemy infiltration in his ministry. I told him many times that witches were on his staff. Though he trusted my judgment, it still did not really settle in to his mind. One day a maintenance man found voodoo paraphernalia planted in the office. There was no question that it was witchcraft. The objects appeared to have been there for years because of the corrosion. One of the objects had the word *DIE* written in large letters on it. My friend's eyes were opened to the reality of infiltration.

Once I found what appeared to be a corroded cantaloupe under the back seat of my personal van. It looked like something from *Star Trek*. I never really figured out what it was. This object had been in my van so long that I had to take a crowbar and pry it from the carpet. Of course, when it finally came up, the carpet was attached to it. I know through experience that witches use fruit as a type of sacrifice. I am sure this object was planted to cause me have an accident. The scary part to me was, who was that close to me to do this? Who had access to me and to my family to this extent? Surely it was an inside job!

I am sure my pastor friend, who has a building with adequate security, wondered the same thing. In both of our cases, no weapons formed against us prospered! This is not always the case. Years ago, I warned one of my ministers of a person who I believed was working voodoo on her. She separated from the person, yet one day insisted on recommitting to the relationship. I told her that I did not feel good about it in my spirit. Though she was perfectly healthy, two weeks later she dropped dead at a young age.

The Bible is true when it declares that we must know those that we labor amongst. I would like to add…and those with whom we hang out.

One of the main avenues that people use to attach witchcraft to their victims is through feeding them. Do not get paranoid about this, but it is good spiritual warfare to know a person by the spirit if that person is feeding you. Let's look at the Word of God on this topic.

> Eat thou not the bread of him that hath an evil eye, neither desire thou his dainty meats: For as he thinketh in his heart, so is he: Eat and drink, saith he to you, but his heart is not with thee. The morsel which thou hast eaten shalt thou vomit up, and lose thy sweet words.
>
> —PROVERBS 23:6, KJV

Pay close attention to the words "evil eye." The word *evil* is *ra* in the Hebrew tongue, and it means "malicious, wretched, harmful, troublesome, adverse, and evil favor." When this word refers to the eye, it is actually talking about the outward appearance. To sum it up, Proverbs 23:6 warns us that we must not eat food from people in whom, by their outward appearance, we can detect evil ways. It is crazy to eat food from people that you know do not like you or your family. The scripture says that if we eat under these circumstances, we will surely get sick. This is a curse!

If obvious enemies can send curses through food, those who can creep in unaware can do the same. The key is this: "As a person thinks, so they are!" If they think evil, they release evil, knowingly or unknowingly. Many understand the power of the tongue in spiritual warfare, but the power of thoughts is just as dangerous when it comes to witchcraft. Why? It is because a lot of the things sent against us are not real; they are images and forms of magnification. Most witchcraft is rooted in the power of meditation. It takes a disciplined mind to intentionally work witchcraft against someone.

Many illnesses are sent through imagery and magnification. This is why people go back to get second opinions from doctors and discover they have no symptoms. It wasn't real in the first place! It was only a demonic image that was sent through thought waves. The truth is that we are healed by the stripes on Jesus' back!

Another case of imagery is symptoms that cannot be diagnosed. People often have serious manifestations of symptoms and pain, but doctors cannot detect anything. This is witchcraft, and it must be dealt with through prayer. If not dealt with, a person can die from undiagnosed symptoms. My cousin died this way. The hospital kept sending her home because they could not diagnose anything. When she died, her children sued the hospital and received a healthy amount of money. This was in Miami, Florida, where voodoo is rampant.

If we receive the lies of images, we will suffer the consequences of them. If we ignore the attacks of the enemy, it will be just as bad. Though the attacks are not naturally real, we must deal with them supernaturally through prayer. A good rule of thumb is to cast down evil images at the inception. What is not cast down will eventually have to be cast out. It may be hard to believe, but there are people who hate you enough to operate as intentional, outright enemies.

David petitioned God for aid against his outright enemies and, according to the following scripture, God takes a strong position against those who devise wickedness in darkness against His people:

> Hear my voice, O God, in my meditation;
> Preserve my life from fear of the enemy.
> Hide me from the secret plots of the wicked,
> From the rebellion of the workers of iniquity,
> Who sharpen their tongue like a sword,
> And bend their bows to shoot their arrows—bitter words,
> That they may shoot in secret at the blameless;
> Suddenly they shoot at him and do not fear.
>
> They encourage themselves in an evil matter;
> They talk of laying snares secretly;
> They say, "Who will see them?"
> They devise iniquities:
> "We have perfected a shrewd scheme."
> Both the inward thought and the heart of man are deep.
>
> But God shall shoot at them with an arrow;
> Suddenly they shall be wounded.
> So He will make them stumble over their own tongue;
> All who see them shall flee away.
> All men shall fear,
> And shall declare the work of God;
> For they shall wisely consider His doing.
>
> The righteous shall be glad in the LORD, and trust in Him.
> And all the upright in heart shall glory.
>
> —PSALM 64:1–10

3. Charismatic witches

The most difficult type of witchcraft for believers to understand is *charismatic witchcraft*. This is witchcraft that subliminally operates through people in the church. The problem is that many do not know what witchcraft really is. Some say they do not believe in witchcraft. To be a Christian and not believe in witchcraft is a great deception. It is to deny the Word of God itself! God is the Creator of all, both good and evil, and He makes reference to both in His Word. If God mentions it in His Word, it is real—even if it is not revealed to us.

The Bible is clear about the topic of witchcraft, and I will use an Old Testament and New Testament scripture to support my point.

First Samuel 15:23 states that "rebellion is as the sin of witchcraft." The first thing that we need to note is that rebellion and witchcraft are the same. The second is that witchcraft is a sin. Rebellion, in this case, actually means bitterness. If bitterness is as the sin of witchcraft, our churches are full of it.

Galatians 5:20 lists witchcraft as a work of the flesh. If witchcraft is a work of the flesh, our churches are full of it.

Witchcraft is deeper than riding on a broomstick or stirring magic potions in a cauldron. It is control, manipulation, rebellion, bitterness, and any work of the flesh that buffets the work of the fruit of the Spirit and the plans of God in our lives. A key point to remember is that the "works of the flesh" are strategically set against the "fruit of the Spirit." Many covet the "gifts" and never pursue the "fruit." This releases the spirit of witchcraft in the church.

Witchcraft is a spirit. The Bible warns us not to give the devil a place (Eph. 4:27). But when we operate ignorantly in the things of the spirit, we release certain things that open doors and give witchcraft a legal right to enter, thus creating the climate for charismatic witchcraft.

Remember that the gifts and the calling of God are irrevocable. (See Romans 11:29.) The word *gifts* is *charisma* in the Greek, and it means "to be endowed with special attributes that makes a person especially gifted." The Bible says that God has given *charisma* freely, and He will not take it back. Even when people leave God and begin living adverse lifestyles, their gifts will continue to operate. This means that a minister can participate in sins that are an abomination to God and still be miraculously used by Him.

These people can move in the gifts of the Spirit, and people will never notice that there is another spirit ministering behind their gift. Charismatic witches can be delivered, but the truth is that many never get set free. They are not aware of the spirit that they are operating in. Because they walk in power, they neglect their own souls. They are deceived into believing that if God continues to use them, they must be all right with Him. This is definitely not the case.

False prophets fall under the category of a charismatic witch. Most false prophets think that they are all right with God. Intercessors who pray prayers by divination also fall under this category. I saw the strongman of intercessory divination; it looked like the praying mantis insect. The word *mantis* means "divination." When intercessors go into the spirit realm, demanding to know things that God is not releasing for them to know, they open up third eyes. When intercessors attempt to control leaders, family members, or any other person through the manipulation of their prayers, it is witchcraft. Jezebel was a control freak, and intercessors must be careful not to submit themselves to her demonic covering. In Galatians 5:20 witchcraft is noted as a work of the flesh. This word *witchcraft* is *pharmekia* in the Greek, and it means "to be magically medicated."

TYPES OF WITCHCRAFT AND DIVINATION

Although white magic and black magic are different in use and nature, both are considered forms of power outside of the Holy Spirit. Those who operate in them are enemies of God, because they operate in illegitimate power. Although people will go to white magic workers (so-called good witches) to break a black magic worker's power (evil witches), white magic is satanic. People who do white magic are called *sons of light*, even though it is a false light.

The devil manifests himself as an angel of light. An example of white magic is when a person manipulates the spirit realm to influence marriage. Many use so-called *love potions,* but in actuality, they are assigning demons to the situation through potion magic. The love potion is only a fetish or a carrier for the demon to ride on. Unfortunately, these kinds of things happen every day. The marriage influences are dedicated to demons and will never have their source in God. Such practice has been called "accursed" and is dedicated to demons (Deut. 7:26). God will not bless the mess.

Black magic is magic done intentionally for evil gain. It can be sorcery, necromancy, the conjuring of spirits, or many other dark acts. The conjuring of spirits or willfully receiving demons for power is the highest level of black magic. People have been dedicated to the magical arts since the beginning of time.

In medieval occultism, witchcraft was classified under seven categories. Every kind of witchcraft imaginable falls under the following categories:

1. Works of light and riches

> For such are false apostles, deceitful workers, transforming themselves into the apostles of Christ. And no wonder! For Satan himself transforms himself into an angel of light. Therefore it is no great thing if his ministers also transform themselves into ministers of righteousness; whose end will be according to their works.
> —2 CORINTHIANS 11:13–15

Everything that looks good is not always good. Those who operate in works of light come in the name of love and good deeds. This is how most cults are formed. The leaders draw innocent, rejected people in the name of false love. God chastens whom He loves. These workers of light usually tell people what they want to hear until they are hopelessly placed under their control. Another kind of work of light is through organizations like Eastern Star and Masonic lodges. These organizations present themselves in the name of the brotherhood or sisterhood. Their cloak of deception is good deeds to the community. A perfect example is the Shriner's hospitals; though they help many children with good deeds, their roots are demonic.

Angels of light have infiltrated the church for years. Everything that is good is not God! If the devil himself is transformed into a false perception of light, our discernment needs to be working overtime. Works of light usually connect with demonic monetary gain.

2. Works of mystery

The power of works of mystery is related to secret council that operates behind the scenes (Ps. 64:2). A secret counsel is an assembly of people in closed deliberation or hidden council. Terrorism is a type of witchcraft, and it falls under works of mystery. Those dedicated to this demonic work vow unto death to do things that cannot be told.

Works of mystery also relate to organizations that make secret vows or dedications of initiation. While some ignorantly join these groups for power and prestige, they fail to realize that they are dedicating their families to demons through initiations. What these groups call *initiation* is actually forms of sacrifice to the devil. These sacrifices open doors to generational curses of witchcraft in family bloodlines. One initiation can affect generations with secret curses that are never revealed. The operation of the Illuminati is the greatest kept secret of all time. This is a group of wealthy people of influence who get what they want done in the world at any cost. Behind the scenes they run the world with secret power. Through acts like theosophy and *theomancy* (the mixture of witchcraft, philosophy, and divination), they tap into realms that defy the natural. I believe that Osama bin Laden is a master spiritualist who operates in this realm. His ability to stay hidden is based on more than natural influence. Through works of mystery demons assist his cover.

3. Works of science or skills

God said He would baffle the minds of the logicians and the statisticians. Many people depend on intellect and their own knowledge.

A perfect example was the biblical Tower of Babel. Genesis speaks of a man named Nimrod. He was the father of Babylonian worship. He was noted as the mighty hunter who came against God. He was the first demi-god, or man, who was worshiped in the earth. The people worshiped him because of his knowledge of science and his skill at the construction of the Tower of Babel. This is witchcraft. Because the Babylonians were placing their dependence upon their own intellect, when they thought they were reaching their highest achievement, God baffled their minds and confused their purpose.

Man's knowledge has tried to reach heaven since the beginning of time. Secular humanists operate under the works of science and skills. To them, knowledge is the only true power, and man is god!

4. Works of retribution and punishment

People who operate in this category of witchcraft are obsessed with participating in the ultimate sacrifice of their bodies. Many cults operate on the principle of receiving punishment and pain as a sacrifice. They walk on nails and pierce and tattoo their bodies. They also submit themselves to fire as a form of repentance. Though some people commit these acts with demonic intentions, there are many who ignorantly act out in works of retribution and punishment. Jesus gave His life for our atonement, and He is the ultimate sacrifice. There is no other! People who attempt to dedicate their lives to become "ultimate sacrifices" come up against the finished work of Christ.

When the prophets of Baal could not get their god to respond on Mt. Carmel, they began to cut themselves (1 Kings 18:28). Cutting, piercing, and marking the body is an ancient demonic ritual. It was considered an act done only by heathens in biblical times. Today, in the form of fads, innocent people pierce and mark their bodies, even Christians. These are fetish acts and very addictive. This is why one earring becomes many, and one tattoo leads to covering the entire body. Every time blood is shed by the piercing of an earring or the pinching of a tattoo needle, it is a sacrifice to the devil. Earring holes are now stretched out to be as big as charm bracelets.

The reason that it gets progressively worse is because demons do not share their space. Their aim is to totally take over. Possession of the entire body is the ultimate goal. In studying ancient cults, it is apparent that we are living in a time when people are starting to look like the people of Sodom and Gomorrah.

5. Works of love

Some churches draw people by false love, which is only a smoke-screen. The goal is ultimate separation. They teach doctrines like, "No one outside of our organization is going to heaven," or "No one can love you like we can." They cause innocent people to separate themselves from their families and loved ones. Though God may cause separation from loved ones for a period, it is demonic when it is manipulated through works of love. The doors that open people up to this kind of witchcraft are rejection, sympathetic magic, and insecurity. The stronghold is a brainwashing spirit.

6. Works of intrigue

This work arouses the curiosity or fascination of a person. Isaiah 19:3 says:

> The spirit of Egypt will fail in its midst;
> I will destroy their counsel,
> And they will consult the idols and the charmers,
> The mediums and the sorcerers.

When Moses threw his rod before Pharaoh it became a snake. The magicians Jannes and Jambres counterfeited Moses' act by tossing two rods that became two snakes. Moses' act was a display of the power of God, but the act of the magicians was a work of intrigue. People are fascinated with the supernatural. We have warlocks on national shows like *Criss Angel (Mindfreak)* that entertain the multitudes with the fascination of witchcraft.

Recently a show was aired on national television where a man attempted to break the world record for holding his breath under water. He had the symbol of Baphomet (the god of the occult world) tattooed on his back. While people saw his act as a circus show, it was a demonic work of intrigue. This man attempted this act by the help of demon powers. I touched and agreed with a few intercessors, and we began to bind his power spirits. Immediately he started choking under the water, and his show was over. The demons that supported him left him in a state of failure and embarrassment.

Just like Houdini, these individuals are modern-day warlocks. What people think to be magical tricks of fun are actually the works of demons through intrigue. It makes the population numb to the truth and receptive to witchcraft while they believe that they are being entertained.

7. Works of malediction and death

This category of witchcraft displays the power of the black arts. Black arts operate when witches provoke evil against people unto death. They are forms of witchcraft incorporated by the spirit of the thief. He comes with the intent to steal, kill, and destroy. Works of malediction and death are utter destructions sent from the dark side.

DIVINATION

Divination is biblically defined as "a soothsaying spirit or the spirit of false prophecy." Below I have listed some of the types of divination. Please note that the suffix *-mancy* means "divination."

- *Aeromancy*—divination by observing atmospheric conditions or ripples on the surface of the water. This is also called water witching.

- *Anthropomancy*—divination by examining the intestines of a dead person, especially in human sacrifices.

- *Apantomancy*—divination by means of an object that happens to meet the eye. (Some people can move objects with their eyes.)

- *Arithmomancy*—fortune-telling by use of numbers.

- *Belomancy*—divination by arrows.

- *Botanomancy*—divination by use of plants and herbs.

- *Cartomancy*—divination by use of cards (example, Tarot cards).

- *Ceromancy*—interpreting shapes and positions assumed by melted wax dropped on the floor.

- *Crystallomancy*—gazing at a mirror or a shiny surface.

- *Crythomancy*—divination by sprinkling flour, especially in connection with sacrificial rites.

- *Daphnomancy*—divination by throwing a laurel branch into fire and interpreting it through the flames.

- *Stolismancy*—divination by wearing articles of clothing a certain way.

- *Halomancy*—A form of divination by using salt.

- *Geomancy*—divination by random figures, formed when a handful of earth is thrown to the ground.

- *Nephelomancy*—divination by observation of the clouds.

- *Necromancy*—the practice of communicating with the dead; also, the practice of predicting the future by communication with the dead.

- *Oniromancy*—divination by dreams and dream books.

- *Rhabdomancy*—the practice of using the divining rod or a divination stick.

- *Clidomancy*—divination by use of the Bible.

- *Chiromancy*—divination by uses of the palms.

- *Bibliomancy*—divination by use of the Scriptures.

- *Lecanomancy*—divination by throwing a stone into a basin of water and interpreting the ripples; sometimes oil is used.

- *Ornithomancy*—a method of divination that interprets the flight patterns of birds; also refers to the divination of the songs of birds. It was a very popular form of divination during ancient Rome where, in fact, it was part of the religion.

- *Tasseomancy*—the art of reading tea leaves; some readers also use coffee grounds.

TYPES OF MAGIC

- *Protective magic*—any act or formula put together to avert or overcome evil.

- *Sympathetic magic*—an occult belief that when a person is separated from someone with whom he or she had a relationship, it can continue to exist through soul ties. This type of magic keeps a link between two individuals even after they are separated. It is a type of long-distance control where natural connection is not necessary. The knot of the tie is self-pity. Even if one party wants to break the tie, self-pity is the glue that keeps it together.

- *Contagious magic*—belief that whatever you come in contact with will have influence on you after you leave (transference of spirits); this can occur through sexual intercourse, drug usage, casual acquaintance, telephones, and television.

- *Defensive magic*—magic used to overcome other magic.

- *Phone voyance*—when people can see through phone lines through supernatural powers.

- *Mimpathy*—to experience the suffering of another; this usually involves pity or sympathy.

- *Clairvoyance*—transcendental vision that gives a person the ability to see in places that they are not physically in contact with.

- *Clairaudience*—transcendental hearing that gives a person a supernatural ability to hear.

- *Clairsentience*—the ability to see things in the spirit by demon powers (false prophecy).

PRAYER TO BREAK WITCHCRAFT

Father, in the name of Jesus, I bind the spirit of the wizard, all Native American witchcraft spirits, and all other territorial witchcraft spirits. I renounce the religious spirit; the spirits of unforgiveness, bitterness, resentment, anger, hate, and spite; the root of bitterness and malice; and any other hindering spirit in my life.

I bind the "third eye" of the mediums, all of their physical, psychic, and spiritual attacks against me and all that concerns me. Every assignment, operation, seeding, work, plan, activity, trap, wile, and snare is bound and blocked from my personal, family, business, and ministry affairs. All curses, hexes, vexes, bewitchments, enchantments, cantrips, ligatures, judgments of witches and warlocks, and acts of evil are cursed to the root.

Witchcraft, sorcery, magic, candle magic, potion magic, black magic, white magic, contagious magic, and omens have no power working against my assignments in life. New Age, Santeria, or Yoruba forces cannot penetrate my barriers of protection. Every working of a curse, ritual, or sacrifice to Satan is counted as null and void.

I plead the blood of Jesus against every act and declare that no weapon formed against me will prosper. All demonic thoughts, threats, mental locutions, statements, and ideations are cast down and will not become strongholds for the devil's use. I renounce all self-inflicted curses through negative confession, imagery, and magnification that I may have opened the doors to. I cancel every demonic strategy against me and the ones I am called to be connected with, covered by, or called to cover. They will never manifest or come to pass and are cursed and destroyed at their root. I render them of no effect. They are judged by God, spoiled, and put to open shame.

Every plan of the enemy will never be seeded into my life and take root. No weapons formed against me will prosper. As soon as the enemy attacks, the reinforcements of the Lord will be launched against him, and his seed dried up. I cast down every vain imagination. It is broken off my ministry, its people, and families immediately, completely, and permanently.

CHAPTER FIVE

Maneuvering in the Spirit

*The Gifts of God to the
Individual Believer*

To MANEUVER IN the Spirit is to flow or move by the Spirit of
God in a tactical manner. The root word for *tactical* is *tact*.
Every believer must be tactful concerning the things of the
Spirit. It is an individual obligation. The opposite of being tactful is to
be reckless. For too long Christians have depended on others who are
considered to be of a higher spiritual authority to move in the Spirit
for them. This will eventually end up in a spiritual collision. They
want to be told what God is saying, and they want someone to get a
revelation of the Word of God for them. Leaders are only supposed
to teach the Word and lead others in the right direction. People have
to get a revelation of and hear from God for themselves. I believe that
leaders should operate as spiritual coaches to teach the masses how to
flow in the things of God.

Many people hire personal trainers to lose weight or get in physical
shape. The trainers show them what to do, but in order to get results,

the individual must do the work. When I ran track, it was very important to me that my coaches had experienced what they were teaching me to do. It is hard to coach someone in what you have never
achieved. My best coaches were people who had firsthand experience
in my field. Not only were they knowledgeable, but they also had a
good track record of doing what they coached me to do.

Despite this, I had to be able to perform on competition day for
myself. The coach's job was to prepare me to use the gift that was
already on the inside of me. A coach cannot make a person who is not
already talented into a champion. Champions are born! God put the
ability for me to be a great sprinter in my belly before the creation of
the world. My coaches identified my gift and taught me how to get
the best results out of it.

I often give my testimony of how I used anabolic steroids at the
end of my track career. I thank God that I never had a chance to win
a major competition with drugs in my body. God saved me as soon as
I started using steroids.

Anabolic steroids made me feel invincible. I would recover almost
immediately after my practice repetitions. I could train harder, so
I got greater results in competition. If a regular person with no
natural athletic ability took these drugs, it would not have the same
affect on them. Steroids only enhance what is already there. What
is my point? Many people are trying to move in things in God
that He did not put in them to do. Like my track coaches, I, as an
apostle, cannot train an individual to do what God has not put in
them to do.

Paul came in contact with Timothy, and through him, gifts that
were lying dormant in Timothy were set ablaze. He released a fire in
Timothy by laying hands on him, and it ignited the call of God on
his life. Timothy's responsibility was to rekindle or stir up that inner
fire (2 Tim. 1:6). This can be done by staying in place to be trained so
that gifts can be sharpened and matured.

First Timothy 4:14–16 (AMP) expounds on this point:

Do not neglect the gift which is in you, [that special inward endowment] which was directly imparted to you [by the Holy Spirit] by prophetic utterance when the elders laid their hands upon you [at your ordination]. Practice and cultivate and meditate upon these duties; throw yourself wholly into them [as your ministry], so that your progress may be evident to everybody. Look well to yourself [to your own personality] and to [your] teaching; persevere in these things [hold to them], for by so doing you will save both yourself and those who hear you.

Training is consistent practice, which cultivates a gift. It promotes progress! The confirmation of ministry gifts that have been set by God is that they progress. God's anointing or confirmation upon them is that people can see the ministry grow from one level to the next. Ministry gifts that lie stagnant and dormant do so because those that have been endowed neglect them. These gifts also lie dormant because leaders do not activate them as they should.

When it comes to the gift of God within a person, I believe if you do not use it, you will lose it! Many people take their gifts to the grave and never experience what God has called them to walk in on earth. They neglect the gift that God has graciously granted them. The word *neglect* in Hebrew is *ameleo*, which means "to disregard and take the gifting of God lightly." As a result, the person becomes reckless with what God has given that person to be a steward over.

First Timothy 1:20 warns us as believers not to be like Hymenaeus and Alexander. They were undisciplined in the things of the Spirit, and their faith was eventually shipwrecked. Hymenaeus was also named with Philetus for being led into deeper ungodliness and teaching messages that devoured people and spread like cancer (2 Tim. 2:17). They were said to have swerved from the truth, undermining the faith of the saints. It appeared that whoever connected with Hymenaeus partook of the curse of his rebellion.

This is an example of the apostasy spoken of in 2 Thessalonians 2:3. This scripture warns of a great falling away that must happen in order for Scripture to be fulfilled. This falling away happens as those who have been truly called by God veer off into deception and end up on the other side. The apostasy is the counterfeit of the apostolic ministry of God. The apostolic sends people forth in God, and apostasy cuts them off and causes them to fall away. The apostolic supports unity and church growth, but apostasy causes division and schism. Just as connecting with the right people will send you forth in your calling, connecting with the wrong ones will cut you off and cause you to miss the mark. Paul finished his course because he kept his eyes on the mark that God had given him in life. Everyone has particular gifts that lead to a certain mark.

First Peter 4:10 (AMP) says:

> As each of you has received a gift (a particular spiritual talent, a gracious divine endowment), employ it for one another as [befits] good trustees of God's many-sided grace [faithful stewards of the extremely diverse powers and gifts granted to Christians by unmerited favor].

I am alarmed when people haphazardly ask me to impart my anointing to them. I do not recklessly deal in the Spirit like that. First of all, I do not see impartation as just giving a person what is on the inside of me. Actually, what is on the inside of them has to connect with what is on the inside of me. Just like Paul, I reach on the inside of others and connect with what God has already placed there. This is what I call *apostolic impartation*. This is the only way that we can multiply our gifts. Many are satisfied with addition when God commanded multiplication. Ten plus ten is twenty, but ten times ten is one hundred. Addition hinders the variety in God; He wants us to be fruitful and multiply! We can only do this by being led by God's Spirit.

BEWARE OF CHARISMATIC WITCHCRAFT

The Bible says that if we are sons of God, we must be led (moved) by the Spirit of God. It is not a popular thing to train people to move by the Spirit in the church. Just as the military trains its soldiers in tactical maneuvers, believers need to be trained to move in the Spirit. They must have spiritual tact. This will promote decency and order and protect the integrity of the warfare and deliverance.

Many have plunged into spiritual warfare indecently and out of order. They were ignorantly uncovered, and the enemy used it to put them to open shame. The end effect is that it brings a reproach to the overall ministry. I have heard the same story for years. People do not want to do warfare because of the experiences they have had with people who did not know how to maneuver in the spirit. In spiritual warfare there are rules of engagement. The cost is great for breaking them.

I pray that the information in this chapter will be a basic training course on how to move in the spirit for you. Once you are trained in anything, it will get down in your spirit and produce habits. Habits are not all bad. We just need to get rid of the bad habits (be delivered) and receive the good habits (be trained). I was a noncommissioned training officer in the army, and my job was to make sure that every soldier had adequate training for his or her area of specialty. The army headquarters had guidelines for each soldier to be trained by according to their job specialty. Nothing could be done outside of those regulations. To move in the things of God it must be done IN GOD! To be in God we have to line up with the ordinances of His Word.

Let's see what the Word of God has to say about this:

> For in Him we live and move and have our being.
>
> —ACTS 17:28

First, we must look at the Greek meanings of the words *live, move,* and *being*.

- *Live—zao,* "to be quickened"

- *Move—kineho,* "to be stirred up to move"

- *Being—esmen,* "to have hope because the gospel has been preached"

To live in God means to be quickened by the Spirit of God. This quickening causes a stirring that makes us move. Webster defines the word *move* as "going from one place to another with a continuous motion." The key to moving in the spirit is continual motion. Things never stand still in the spirit. They are always moving!

The million-dollar question is this: In what direction are they moving? When we maneuver in the spirit, we move toward the things of light, or we move toward the things of darkness. This means that people can move in the spirit *outside of God.* All spiritual movement is not "in God." When people in the church move outside of God, I call it charismatic witchcraft. We have many gifted men and women of God in the body of Christ. The Bible tells us that their gifts are irrevocable. In other words, God does not take them back! Because He does not take spiritual gifts back, people can continue to move in the spirit outside of God. This chapter teaches foundational principles on moving in the spirit. It is a safeguard against charismatic witchcraft in the church.

The Greek word for *move* is *kineho.* It is related to the English word *kinetics.* Kinetics is the study of motion or movement. When we accept Jesus in our lives, only then do we have our own being! In Him we live, move, and have our being. After we accept Jesus, we can begin to move legally in the spirit. Having our own being in God safeguards us from illegitimate movement in the spirit.

What is illegitimate movement in the spirit? Let's use the example of illegal driving violations in the natural. It is illegal to drive without a license, but this does not stop people from breaking the law. They drive around doing things that they have not been tested and licensed for. As believers, we must be apostolically released and continually covered to walk in certain realms of the spirit. We must deal with the lawlessness in the church when people break spiritual laws and "drive" without a license.

Many do not *wait* on God, and they run red lights when He tells them to stop. Without *looking* where they are going, they cut over into the lanes of other saints and cause spiritual collisions. They do not *yield* when God warns them to. They are bold to keep going when God is directing them to get off the next exit. They ignore the *detours* of God that take them out of their way because it seems faster to keep going. They fail to realize that God's way may take longer, but it will prevent many spiritual accidents along the way. (See Exodus 13:17.)

The Bible warns us that there is a way that seems right to our flesh, but the end of it is death (Prov. 14:12). The root word for *gifts* is the Greek word *charisma*. It is dangerous to be led by gifts. Without the intervention of the Holy Spirit, gifts always promote the things of the flesh. The strength of charismatic witchcraft is the work of the flesh! It is not the power of the witchcraft it possesses, but the power of men to yield to their flesh. When we are led by the prompting of the flesh over the unction of the Holy Ghost, it will always lead to death. The flesh will always maintain the "right of way," even when it has none. It thrives to satisfy its own lustful desires.

Those who choose to maintain their way of doing things and continue to break the laws of the "roads of the Spirit" will receive warnings. If they do not heed these warnings, they will eventually be pulled over and taken to spiritual jail.

I meet people all of the time who minister in spiritual bondage. They *see* things in the spirit and use their spiritual gifts, but they are not rooted in God. They prophesy, interpret dreams, and just "know" things, but they do not know God.

I have been in many conversations with people who confess that they *knew things* supernaturally before they were saved. Anything that people see in the spirit outside of God is only seen through a third eye. A third eye was opened up in the garden when Adam and Eve ate the forbidden fruit. The Bible says that their eyes were opened. They already had two natural eyes, so this means that a spiritual third eye was opened. They were tapping into what God did not want them to see.

A third eye is located on the center of the forehead in the spirit. It is a place of ignorant demonic spiritual insight or intentional rebellion. Many witches use the power of the third eye to defy God. Uninformed individuals who have accessed the demonic power through a third eye, and then come to Jesus and are saved, may continue to operate in the power of the third eye behind the scenes. Most leaders do not have a clue for how to deal with them. Many of these people grow through the ranks of the church to become pastors, apostles, and bishops. They innocently flow in the things of the spirit through third eyes. Despite their innocent intentions, dark forces continue to operate behind the scenes through their gifts. This is charismatic witchcraft! God warned us that His people perished for a lack of knowledge. We must pray for every gift in the house of God to be dedicated unto Him. We can close third eyes so that the eyes of our understanding will be enlightened and the hope of His calling for our lives manifested (Eph. 1:18).

BEING QUICKENED TO MOVE

My testimony has changed lives around the world. Through my book *Delivered to Destiny* people have experienced a spiritual change from the prisons to the political arenas of the world.[1] I have many accolades before Christ, but they did not mean anything until I got *in Christ*. Who I was, what I did, or where I had been had no true meaning until I got in Christ!

When the gospel was preached to me, I began to "be." In Him I obtained my being. What I am outside of Him does not even count. This is a very important revelation to have when you are moving in the spirit. Repeat these words: OUTSIDE OF GOD I AM NOTHING!

This is the power of moving in the spirit, acknowledging our nothingness in comparison to His awesomeness!

When I was praying about this chapter, I heard the Lord say clearly, "It is 'not by might nor by power, but by My Spirit'" (Zech. 4:6). The word *power* in this passage is *koakh* in the Hebrew, and it means "to have the ability to get wealth." This is the same word in Deuteronomy 8:18, which refers to the power to get wealth. The word *might* is *chayil*, which means "to be virtuous and war worthy." *Chayil* is the same word used for the virtuous woman in the Book of Proverbs. It is clear that God wants us to have virtue and the power to get wealth. The point Zechariah was making is that to be in God is not just about power, wealth, and might. To have these things and never have the Spirit of God is futile. We must be quickened to move by the Spirit of God.

In the Old Testament, the word *spirit* is called the *ruwach*. *Ruwach* means "breath or wind of God." When God created Adam, He blew *ruwach* into him. Adam was just a lump of dirt until he received the *ruwach*. That is what we are without God, just a lump of dirt! After Adam received the *ruwach*, he began to exist.

Genesis speaks of "the cool of the day." This word *cool* is also *ruwach*. There is a wind of God that we can walk in throughout our days. It is a terrible thing when we attempt to walk out our days without the *ruwach* of God.

The spirit of pride makes a man attempt to walk out his days without God's Spirit. Let's take a look at Job 41:15–17:

> His rows of scales are his pride,
> Shut up tightly as with a seal;
> One is so near to another
> That no air can come between them;
> They are joined one to another.
> They stick together and cannot be parted.

This scripture is referring to Leviathan, the king of the children of pride. We know that pride is a spirit, so we can safely say that

Leviathan is not just a natural creature, but a spirit. The word *air* is also *ruwach* in the Hebrew. The scales of the back of Leviathan are described as being like rows of metal shields. These are the protective shields of pride that will not let the Spirit of God in. These scales or shields are so tightly put together that no air or revival can get in.

To be revived means to be resuscitated or to get a fresh breath. When believers walk in pride, the condition reinforces itself, and revival is impossible. They are doomed to never receive a release, and the air of God is cut off from them. God resists the proud! Pride spiritually stifles a man, and *no air can get in.* I believe that this is why God declares in Joel 2:29 that He will pour out His Spirit (*ruwach)* on all flesh. The *ruwach* that the prophet Joel spoke of in the Old Testament manifested in the New Testament as the *pneuma.*

From the beginning God wanted us to walk in the cool of the day. Surely in the last days we must have His Spirit even more. This is what the restoration of the church is all about. One of the definitions for restoration is to be put back into existence. Prayer warriors must understand that they must be in God to do spiritual warfare. Reader, if you are embarking upon spiritual warfare outside of Him, let's deal with it now! If you are not in Him, I prophesy that the Spirit of the Lord is dealing with you now. Do not allow religious or self-righteous spirits to talk you out of what the Lord is saying to you now. Let's pray:

> *Father God, in the name of Jesus, I repent for trying to deal in the spirit out of the Spirit of God. I recognize that I have been shooting with a weapon that is about to backfire on me, and I lay it down. I renounce the spirit of pride and any other hindering or blocking spirits that would get me out of my place in God. Lord, thank You for total restoration! What the devil has meant for evil is turning around for my good now.*

Praise the Lord! Now we are ready to move forward! We are the forces of the Lord, and we want to be fully equipped to be on the front lines. Winds of End-Time restoration are blowing so that the forces of the Lord will get in place. This is what happened in Ezekiel 37.

> The hand of the LORD came upon me and brought me out *in the Spirit of the LORD*, and set me down in the midst of the valley; and it was full of bones.
>
> —EZEKIEL 37:1, EMPHASIS ADDED

Ezekiel was allowed to go into the spirit. The word *carried* means to be sent with a commandment. Ezekiel was on apostolic assignment; he was a sent one! In verse 9 he was commanded to prophesy to the wind (*ruwach*). He was told to command that the four winds of the *ruwach* would come forth and breathe (send the *ruwach*) upon those that were slain.

Many intercessors are living in the valley of dry bones because they have been slain. They need revival! These dry bones represent that which was unproductive and lying dormant. Even though the bones were dead, there must have been potential in them, or God would have never told the prophet to prophesy to them. Just because things appear to be dead does not mean it is over. God has given us the power to decree and declare to dead things to live. When we do this, the devil is under a mandate to "give it back" even after it had been pronounced dead. This is one of the highest levels of warfare, raising the dead! God knows that we need to raise dead prayer lives! I prophesy to the ears of the readers of this book that need revival in their prayer lives. In the name of Jesus, rise up and be the valiant force in the earth realm that God has called you to be!

Statistics are scary concerning how much praying is really going on. I know that God has a remnant, and I am in no way saying that He does not. I am only addressing the fact that there is a spirit of prayerlessness in the church that has not been addressed. I am not speaking about prayer over the microphones where everyone can hear. I am addressing prayer behind the scenes. How many are really standing in the gaps? We need a fresh breath of *ruwach* to blow from the four corners of the earth so that an army can be raised up to stand in the gap.

Over the years there have been many great moves of God. The move that we need to get our stuff out of the enemy's camp is corporate prayer revival. It is time for the dead bones of the church to stand up and thrive in intercession and warfare.

Let's continue to read from Ezekiel 37.

> So I prophesied as He commanded me, and breath came into them, and they *lived*, and stood upon their feet, an exceedingly great army.
>
> —EZEKIEL 37:10, EMPHASIS ADDED

Wow! Ezekiel prophesied to dead bones, and they did not just come alive, they became a great army. Will you stand in the gap for the valley of dry bones of intercessors and prayer warriors in the church? Let me explain the difference between an intercessor and a prayer warrior. In the natural army, there are general enlisted soldiers and special forces. Prayer warriors are the special forces of the Lord. Just as the dead bones had to be quickened, people must be quickened to the call of the intercessor and prayer warrior.

In verse 14 God promised to put His Spirit (*ruwach*) in this great army and place them in their own land. Once we are in Him, we get in place! There is nothing like being in place. I call it, "my place called *There*." When Jehoshaphat moved out of place with God, his solution was simple: "Get back in place with God." God sent the prophet to tell him to go to the Ascent of Ziz (a place—2 Chron. 20:16). God also told Joshua that as long as he remained in the place that He had given him, the land belonged to him. As a result of this, his enemies could not stand before him (Josh. 1:4–5).

We must pray according to the Word and the will of God. But we must not forget that it is our position in the spirit realm that fuels the ignition for prayers that produce results.

EFFECTUAL FERVENT PRAYER

James 5:16 teaches: "The effective, fervent prayer of a righteous man avails much." This confirms what we have been studying in this chapter. There is a place we must be to release prayers that produce results. It is called *right standing with God*. I have done a word study on this passage. Let's look at these definitions:

- *Effectual:* Prayers that produce the desired results. The root word is *effect*, which means "power that has influence and brings results."

- *Fervent:* Zealous, earnest, hot-off-the-press prayer that is so on fire that it spreads and catches hold of everything it comes in contact with.

- *Avail:* Prayers that have advantages or benefits by praying them.

Based on the definitions above we can sum up James 5:16 by saying that our prayers must release power that has influence, benefit, and advantage to produce results. The opposite of releasing effectual prayer is praying amiss. Sometimes we take praying amiss lightly. It is a serious sin in the eyes of God! The word *amiss* is *kakos* in the Greek, and it literally means to pray evil prayers.

> You ask and do not receive, because you ask amiss, that you may spend it on your pleasures.
>
> —JAMES 4:3

Oh, how we have misinterpreted this scripture in the church. Many would say that this scripture means that we do not have what we need because we have not asked for it. Not so! This verse actually means that we have been asking, but we are asking *out of the will of God*. The Bible does say that the Lord will give us the desires of our hearts, but God gave me a specific revelation about this. (See Psalm 37:4.)

When I was first saved I had an experience with the Lord concerning this. God was answering my prayers so quickly that I was actually concerned. I appreciated His love and all He did for me, but I did not know anyone else for whom He was moving as He was moving for me. One day I asked God why He was moving on my behalf like He was.

God told me that He appreciated how I had given up everything for Him. There was not a person, place, or thing that I would not have given up for God. I met Jesus, and it flipped every script in my life. I wish that I could bottle what I felt and give it away. People did not understand, and, guess what—it did not matter! God went on to tell me that when I had given up everything, He took the desires of those things away from me and replaced them with His desires. He said to me, "You see, when I answer your prayers, I am only answering My will for you!"

This revelation has never left my heart. I have since then prayed that God would remove any desires from my heart that did not line up with His will for my life. I came to grips with the fact that God knows what is best for me. When the Word says that He gives us the desires of our hearts, it has a deeper meaning to me. God does not just answer the prayers that are already in my heart. He removes anything that is not His will for me and literally *gives me the desires* of my heart. It is as though God is answering His own prayers for me. This is perfect prayer—the perfect will of God!

When Jesus interceded, He did not pray His will but the will of the Father. Motives are very important to God when it comes to prayer. When we are praying, God does not just hear *our words,* but He also looks at *our hearts.* Jesus did not pray selfish prayers. He gave Himself to the purpose of the kingdom. His intercession was kingdom-centered and not self-centered. When James accused the people of praying amiss, he said they were trying to consume their own lusts (James 4:3, KJV). *Lust* is a serious word. It is a type of desire that has no bottom to it. It is never satisfied! To be never satisfied is the curse spoken of in Haggai.

"You looked for *much*, but indeed it came to little; and when you brought it home, I blew it away. Why?" says the LORD of hosts. "Because of My house that is in ruins, while every one of you runs to his own house."

—HAGGAI 1:9, EMPHASIS ADDED

The people in Haggai's day looked for much to come in. This is what the spirit of lust does. It always wants much! They overlooked the needs in God's house and were only concerned about their own "ceiled" houses (v. 4, KJV). The word *ceiled* means fashioned and put in order.

Haggai addressed this selfish group of people because they spent all their time and effort on their own homes and did not want to build the Lord's house. They said it was not time, but the real issue was that they were selfish and full of lust. Lust is self-gratifying and never considers anyone else.

I could imagine that these people of this era suffered great loss. God was not pleased with them. I am so glad Haggai did not respond to this like some ministers today would have. Instead of beating around the bush with them, he told them that they needed to "consider their ways" (v. 7). He assured them that their loss was not caused by the devil but by God. God blew another wind toward them. It is called *naphach* in the Hebrew. This wind was blown by God, and it disesteemed and caused life to be lost. It also scattered, expired, and snuffed out. We do not hear many messages preached from our pulpits today on the *naphach*. Whether it is preached or not, it exists!

Praying amiss has nothing to do with a lack of prayer; it is about wrong prayers. The Greek word *kakos* also means to pray prayers that are diseased, grievous, and sick in the eyes of God. In warfare prayer and intercession we cannot pray haphazardly. "Any way the wind blows is cool with me" prayers are not cool with God. They will send the wrong breeze our way. As for me and my house, we are getting in place to receive the *ruwach* and not the *naphach*!

God is bringing restoration to intercessory prayer in the last days, especially in America! Out of this intercessory prayer movement, prayer warriors will be birthed. Before people become intercessors, they must first develop a healthy relationship with God. This will promote prayer lives that will not be sick and diseased in the eyes of God. People must spend enough time with God to be able to know what He likes and dislikes. After this, they can become prayer warriors and be released to the front lines. Generally speaking, prayer warriors must be seasoned, disciplined, and mature. Of course, there is always the exception to the rule in God. He can raise a prayer warrior from the dirt. That is all we are anyway.

STANDING IN THE GAP

There is a sound being released in the spirit that is putting saints on spiritual alert. This sound will bring forth a burden in the hearts of men and women to stand in the gap for real! What does it mean to *stand in the gap*? The word *gap* is *perets* in the Hebrew, and it means to make a breach and cause to break away. A breach is a place where an infraction of a law or standard has occurred, and there has been a breaking of friendly relations. Standing in the gap is not about making friends! It is waging war and declaring every thing illegal that the enemy is trying to make legal. When we stand in the gap we literally get between the devil and whatever he is attempting to do and declare it illegitimate. There is no such thing as standing in the gap without doing warfare. The gap is a place of warfare, and this will never change.

God addressed standing in the gap in two passages:

> You have not gone up into the gaps to build a wall for the house of Israel to stand in battle on the day of the LORD.
>
> —EZEKIEL 13:5

> And I sought for a man among them, that should make up the hedge, and stand in the gap before me for the land, that I should not destroy it: but I found none.
>
> —EZEKIEL 22:30, KJV

Not only are we called to stand in the gap, but we are also called to make up the hedge. The word *hedge* is *gader,* and it is defined as the wall. We need prayer warriors that will commit to get back up on the walls. This is how we make up the hedge; we make a difference! How? By rebuilding the prayer walls in the twenty-first century that the enemy has burned down in the years past.

We must fill in the spaces of intercession so that the devil will have no room to thrive. The gaps, the walls, and the gates of the church are being set in order. Orders are being sent out to gatekeepers and watchmen to control the spiritual airways. God is anointing *roving guards* with apostolic authority to man perimeters of the spirit realm assigned to them. They will not be distracted by a set position, and they will have the ability to shift into prayer assignments as the Lord requires. They will be known as gap dwellers, wall watchers, and gatekeepers. They will maneuver in the spirit and prompt others to follow them! Leaders who are hungry for the power of God are training intercessors to become twenty-first-century soldiers for the Lord. There is a clarion call coming from the Word of the Lord in 2 Chronicles 7:14–15:

> If My people who are called by My name will humble themselves, and pray and seek My face, and turn from their wicked ways, then I will hear from heaven, and will forgive their sin and heal their land. Now My eyes will be open and My ears attentive to prayer made in this place.

Will you answer the call?

CHAPTER SIX

The Armor of God

The Wiles of the Enemy

BASIC TRAINING WAS quite an experience for me. When the recruiter picked me up to go to the processing center to be inducted into the army, I was smoking cocaine. I was peeping out of the window telling him I was coming as I was hitting a crack pipe. As you probably could imagine, my transition from the streets to basic training was quite drastic. Upon my arrival to basic training, the army's first challenge in turning me into a soldier was making me look like one.

New recruits were taken to a big warehouse that had an assembly line. We were given everything we needed to be clothed as a soldier. They gave us boots, hats, belts, and uniforms. Before we went to the assembly line, orders were given to us to authorize uniform pick up. It is the same in Ephesians 6:11 where believers are given spiritual orders to put on the armor of God. It declares that we must put on the whole armor. *Holokleros* is a Greek word for *whole*. It means "complete in every part, leaving nothing out, or to be perfectly sound." Our warfare cannot be perfectly sound unless we use every part of the armor of God described in Ephesians 6.

The purpose for the armor of God is very clear.

> Put on the whole armor of God, that you may be able to stand against the wiles of the devil.
>
> —EPHESIANS 6:11

The foundational purpose for the armor of God is clear. It gives us the power to stand against the wiles of the enemy in the midst of evil days. The Bible speaks of wiles in the Old and New Testaments of the Bible.

OLD TESTAMENT MEANING OF WILES

> For they vex you with their wiles, wherewith they have beguiled you in the matter of Peor, and in the matter of Cozbi, the daughter of a prince of Midian, their sister, which was slain in the day of the plague for Peor's sake.
>
> —NUMBERS 25:18, KJV

In the Book of Numbers it mentions the matter of Peor. This matter referred to Baal Peor, known as the "lord of the opening." This is the idol that stopped twenty-four thousand of the children of Israel from entering into the Promised Land because they worshiped this idol. It was more than a lack of faith—they were in idolatry! This scripture also shows that the Midianites vexed the people of God with their wiles.

The Hebrew word for *wiles* is *nekel.* It means:

- Treachery
- Conspiracy
- Beguilement
- Subtle

- Deceit
- Trickery
- Deception

Spirits that came in the form of idols tricked the people of God into idolatry. Most idolatry is rooted in fetishism. A fetish is an object with a demon attached to it.

To be subject to the wiles of the enemy means to be deceived. Few people willingly worship the devil. His methods blind their minds into making them think that they are doing anything but worshiping. Worship is what the warfare is all about. God desires our worship, but the devil wants to be worshiped as well.

One of the greatest scenes of warfare in the Bible was when the devil took Jesus to the top of the mountain during His wilderness experience. He asked Jesus to worship him, yet he offered him things of the world. When we accept the things of the world from the devil, it is the highest form of worship. Worship is not just *what we do* but *what we abstain from doing*! When we accept the offers of the devil, it is a type of Baal Peor that opens demonic doors in the spirit realm. Most believers are trying to serve God, so the enemy has to use deceiving methods to make them worship him ignorantly. Paul called it the *altar of the unknown god* (Acts 17:23). Paul said they ignorantly worshiped at this altar.

NEW TESTAMENT MEANING OF "WILES"

In the New Testament, the word *wiles* is *methodeia* in the Greek. Though it is related to the English word *method*, it actually means "to operate under a traveling cover and to *lie in wait*." This is the foundation truth of the wiles of the devil—to lie behind the scenes and watch a person until a vulnerable moment arises so that he can attack. It is important that we review the word *method*. It is:

- A technique
- An art
- A system
- The ways
- The skills
- The disciplines
- The habitual practices
- The patterns
- The classifications
- The plans
- The orderly arrangements

All of these are used by the satanic kingdom to deceive man and keep him out of place with God! It is not new; it started in the Book of Genesis.

> And I will put enmity between you and the woman, and between your offspring and her Offspring {Jesus}; He will bruise and tread your head underfoot, *and you will lie in wait and bruise his heel.*
>
> —Genesis 3:15, AMP, emphasis added

THE WILES OF THE ENEMY AGAINST THE BLACK MAN IN AMERICA

In Genesis 3:15 God was speaking directly to the devil. He told the devil that Jesus would bruise his head underfoot and that he would bruise Jesus' heel. This word *heel* is *aqueb* in the Hebrew, and it means "to lie in wait." *Aqueb* comes from another Hebrew word, *aquab*. This word means "to seize by the heel and cause to be restrained." I have prepared an in-depth teaching on this principle in the demonic plan against the black male seed in America. It is called "Lier in Wait." Just as described in Genesis, the enemy lies in wait to bruise the heels of the black male seed. I realize the enemy wants every soul, but the purpose of my point is to address the assignment against young black men in America.

I have found the teaching on "The Lier in Wait" to be an effective tool in bringing black men out of prisons and off the streets. It simply exposes the wiles of the enemy and lets the brothers know what they are really dealing with. They get a revelation that they have to be removed from under the power of the system that is designed to work against them. The reinforcing power of this system is strengthened when they do not know who their enemy really is.

It cannot be denied that systems are set in place in America whereby black men are allocated to lose before they ever begin. It takes more for a black man to be free under natural circumstances and situations than a white man. I know that these are strong words, but we must deal with *how it is*!

The root of this problem stems from the spirit realm and not the natural realm. Because it is a spiritual assignment, there are no natural solutions. I believe that our effectiveness in saving black men from the disasters of the streets, prison, and, ultimately, the grave is in teaching them who their enemy really is. Once they get this revelation, it is an entirely whole new ball game. Their enemy is not the white man! It is the prince of darkness, the lier in wait, who grabs the black man by his heels in life and holds him back. God has given us power over what the enemy is doing behind the scenes! Once he is busted out...it is over!

Because many black men have not been taught who their enemy really is, pro-black cult groups are brainwashing young black men on our college campuses. We need prayer warriors from the black community who will infiltrate the black college campuses so that effective evangelism can take place.

The root of the problem with black males in America is not employment, education, or even the "fatherless rate." God has said that He will be a father to the fatherless, so it could not be this (Ps. 68:5). I believe that it is "the Godless rate." Because of the lack of God in homes, few fathers are present.

You may ask, "Are you saying that more white people are serving God than black people?" Absolutely not! I am saying that Satan is a strategist, and this is his strategy or wile against the black male in America. As black people, we have our demons, and white folks have theirs. Demons travel through the airways of bloodline curses, and if we are in a same race, we will have to deal with similar battles. Black men in America can overcome the wiles of the enemy when they recognize who their enemy really is and his methods against them.

PUTTING ON THE WHOLE ARMOR

I notice that the armor of God is not for special or set-apart saints for spiritual warfare. It is not for fivefold ministry gifts. Ephesians 6:10 says, "Finally, my *brethren*, be strong in the Lord and in the power of His might." The verse indicates that the armor of God is for "the brethren." This means it is simply for those who are saved and blood bought. Every person in the body of Christ should be putting on the whole armor of God!

Ephesians 6:12 identifies who the battle is against:

- Principalities
- Powers
- Rulers of the darkness of this age
- Spiritual wickedness in high places

Verse 13 reminds us that the days will be evil. This means that as a believer, you will be under attack. The whole armor of God helps us to ward off the attacks of the enemy. Ephesians 6:14–18 explains the details of what every part of the armor is and what its purpose is.

The passage begins by telling us to stand and put on our armor. This word *stand* is very important, because it means "to be established in covenant." The Greek word is *histemi,* and it means "to abide in established covenant." When we stand, we abide in the covenant promises of God. Putting on the whole armor of God is a part of this covenant. God's covenant promise to us is that no matter how mad the devil gets, and how evil times get, God will keep and protect us.

The significance of the whole armor of God is that no part works alone. If you have your feet shod with peace and do not have on the helmet of salvation, it is futile. Every piece of the armor has been given to us by God to wear in evil days. Personally, I find it easier to start from the top of my head to the bottom of my feet when I put on my armor. After I am spiritually dressed (head to toe), I take up the sword of the Spirit and the shield of faith and go forth equipped for the evil day.

Let's review each part of the armor of God.

THE WHOLE ARMOR OF GOD

Part of Armor	Covering Assignment	Our Help
Helmet of Salvation	Mind	Helps us to stay saved
Breastplate of Righteousness	Heart	Helps us to be in right standing with God
Belt of Truth	Loins	Helps us to abstain from living lies and protects us from sexual impurity
Shoes of the Gospel of Peace	Feet	Helps us to be in the peace that the gospel has given us, to keep the devil underfoot, and to be led by God

Part of Armor	Covering Assignment	Our Help
Sword of the Spirit	Our offense/defense	Helps us in war and judicial punishment
Shield of Faith	Our defense	Protects us by shutting the doors of the enemy
Praying in the Spirit	Our offense/defense	Builds up our most holy faith and helps us to war against the unknown

The list above is a visual of the operation of the whole armor of God in our lives. Each part of the armor has an assigned covering. It covers our mind, heart, loins, and feet. It also covers our offensive and defensive positions against the enemy in the spirit. The revelation that I received on each piece of armor came from my study of the meaning of each part of armor based on the Greek word meanings.

The helmet

The word *helmet* in our armor of salvation is *perikephaiaia* in the Greek, and it means to encircle and protect the head. When we wear the helmet of salvation, it empowers us for continual renewal of the mind. The mind is a spiritual battlefield, and without the helmet of salvation it is impossible to have a victorious life in Christ Jesus.

When I was in the military, going outside of a building without a head covering was unheard of. I was literally brainwashed to believe that this was unacceptable. The strategy was that if your head was not covered in wartime, the enemy could easily detect you from above and target you for attack. This is why our caps and helmets were made to fit in with the scenery, so that enemy forces flying above our heads could not identify us. The prince of the power of the air can easily identify believers who do not wear the helmet of salvation. I am convinced that people who end up in backslidden states took their helmet off at some point.

The breastplate

The breastplate of righteousness covers the chest. In the days of the Roman soldiers, true warriors wore a breastplate for battle. This part of the armor is very important because it covers the heart. The fastest way to take a person out is to stab him in the heart. To be righteous means to be in right standing with God. To do this we must guard our hearts!

The word *breast* is *thorax* in the Greek. It means to wear a corset or plate about the breast. I have a sister who is a police officer in Jacksonville, Florida. I can easily relate the breastplate to her bulletproof vest. When she is on duty, she is never without it! She is a uniformed officer, and that means she can be easily identified. At any time she can walk into a dangerous altercation and be under fire.

Because we do not know when the enemy will attack, I believe that we should put on the whole armor of God every day. Surely we need the breastplate daily to guard our hearts. Witchcraft flows fluently through dirty hearts! A dirty heart is a heart that is not right with God. Dirty hearts create wrong spirits. I have met prayer warriors who were powerful but had wrong spirits. They got off course by allowing the wrong seeds to be planted in their hearts. David was a great prayer warrior! He prayed, "Create in me a clean heart…and…a right spirit" (Ps. 51:10, KJV).

The belt of truth

The next part of armor is the belt of truth. Jeanna Thomlinson, a pastor in Jacksonville, Florida, wrote a book on loin truth and asked me to come to her church and minister on the topic. Oh how we need loin truth in the church today! The Bible says that our loins should be girt about with truth. This word *girt* in the Greek is *perizonnumi,* and it means "to be fastened with a belt."

I do not think that it is by chance that this is the part of the armor that covers our private parts. It is only the truth that can keep even a believer sexually pure. I have met with some of the greatest men and women of God, and they have admitted either to being trapped or almost trapped by seducing spirits. The name of the strongman assigned against ministers of the gospel to draw them into sexual perversion is *Enticer*. How do I know? Everything cannot be explained by Greek and Hebrew word studies or by *Webster's Dictionary*. I know this by the Spirit of God, and if it agrees with your spirit, use it. If it does not, just take it as my opinion.

Enticer is a spirit that lures the souls of men into perversions and sucks righteousness out of them. It is a demon that travels back and forth from the pits of hell in the forms of beauty, power, and need. Enticer will fulfill the need of every fantasy lust. To those who cannot get their needs met in God, the enticing spirit will lure them into temporary fulfillment. The problem is that it only lasts a minute, and the end is death.

Let's look at the fall of mankind. The death that Adam and Eve experienced was not natural. They lived hundreds of years after the Fall. In Genesis 2:25 (before the Fall), they were both naked. It is interesting that after they fell, the Bible declares their nakedness as if they never were earlier. (See Genesis 3:7.) Apparently this was a different kind of nakedness. This is confirmed in *Strong's Exhaustive Concordance.* The word *naked* in Genesis 2:25 is *arowm,* and it simply means to have no clothes on. The word *naked* in Genesis 3:7 (after the Fall) has a new meaning. It is *eyrom* in the Hebrew and comes from another Hebrew word, *aram.* This word means "to be made bare."

In other words, this nakedness was under an influence outside of God. This nakedness was not the natural nakedness in which God had created them and that meant "to be exposed and uncovered." This nakedness meant "to be removed from under the covering of God." The nakedness that came upon them in their sinful nature is also explained in the Hebrew interpretation as cunning and subtle. They had taken on the nature of a serpent.

We do not have to be uncovered in the private areas of our lives, especially when it comes to sexual purity! God gave us a way out before the enemy ever laid his snare. If you are a man or a woman bound by sexual impurity, repent and go the other way! Girt your loins about with truth, and walk out of the stronghold that Enticer has tailored for you. Just as the enemy had a tailor-made trap, God has tailor-made deliverance for you!

I am going to keep it real: you will need support. After you pray the prayer that follows, contact someone whom you can trust. If you attempt to walk out your deliverance alone, the enemy will snuff you out. God has someone for you! You need to seek counseling, deliverance, and accountability.

In the name of Jesus, I bind…

- Fornication
- Pornography
- Incest
- Molestation
- Masturbation
- Homosexuality
- Lesbianism
- Adultery
- Sexual fantasy and lust
- Nightmares from Incubus and Succubus spirits
- Sexual orgies
- Addictions to strip clubs and prostitutes
- All other forms of perversion

Call out the assignments that have been set against you! Now, read this prayer aloud!

Father God, I renounce every attack against my loins. I announce loin truth! My loins are girt about with truth, and I will not be left naked and ashamed. Holy Spirit, You are my keeper. Open the doors of counseling, deliverance, and accountability in my life. I separate myself from every person, place, or thing that would be a trigger to sexual perversion in my life. I am free from every enticing and seducing spirit.

Lord, I thank You that this bondage is no longer a snare to my soul. Any spirits that have been assigned to my children (by generational curses) through acts that I have committed are cursed to the root and cannot flow through my lineage. In Jesus' name, I decree and declare that my generations are walking in loin truth. Amen.

Shoes of the gospel of peace

It is important that our feet are shod with the gospel of peace. The steps of a just man are led by the Lord. The Bible says that though he may fall seven times, he will get up every time (Prov. 24:16). This is the covenant that we have with God concerning covering our steps. We may make some mistakes, but God ultimately delivers us into victory. When the Book of Ephesians speaks of the gospel of peace, the word *peace* is the Greek word *eirene.* It means to join with peace, rest, and prosperity, and be set at one again. When we shod our feet with the preparation of the gospel of peace, it prepares a path for our way to be prosperous. Not only is there a rest released, but we are "set at one" with the will of God for our lives. It is a dangerous thing to attempt to walk out the will of God without this part of the armor of God.

The sword of the Spirit

The sword of the Spirit is an offensive *and* defensive weapon. The word *sword* is *machaira* in the Greek, and it is defined as an instrument of war for judicial punishment. It is related to another Greek word, *mache,* and this word is used to convey controversy, fighting, and striving. The sword of the Spirit is a weapon used for war! Weapons are made to attack and to protect. A sword can be used to stab or to stop a blow. Though this part of the armor is offensive in nature, it also has a defensive operation. Ephesians 6:17 declares that the sword of the Spirit is the Word of God. This is the part of the Word of God that judges our enemies. In biblical times God brought the sword upon the land to judge the enemies of His people. This was the case with Babylon. (See Ezekiel 33:2.) We do not use the Word to judge our enemies, but when we carry the sword in obedience, our enemies are automatically judged by the Word of God.

The shield of faith

The shield of faith, or *thureos*, is described in the Greek as a large door-shaped shield in the spirit. Based on this, I believe we can say that when we use the shield of faith, it closes doors to our enemies. Ephesians 6:16 says that, above all, we should take the shield of faith so that the fiery darts of the wicked will be quenched. This is a very important part of our defense in spiritual warfare. A shield covers and protects. Without this part of armor, doors can be opened to ignite the darts of evil in our lives.

Praying in the Spirit

The most overlooked part of the armor of God is "praying in the Spirit." Many do not see this as part of the armor of God. Ephesians 6:18 (AMP) reads:

> Pray at all times (on every occasion, in every season) in the Spirit, with all [manner of] prayer and entreaty. To that end keep alert and watch with strong purpose and perseverance, interceding in behalf of all the saints (God's consecrated people).

Many powerful points come from this passage:

1. Pray at all times, every occasion and season.
2. Pray with all manners of prayer.

3. Stay alert and watch with strong purpose and perseverance.
4. Intercede on the behalf of God's consecrated people.

To sum it up, this is the part of the armor that we use offensively, but it becomes a defense to those for whom we stand in the gap. As we release a weapon of prayer, our enemies will be shut down. Have you ever thought of prayer as a part of the armor of God? Well, it is!

Ephesians refers to "all manners of prayer." This means that we have to pray in every biblical manner, especially "praying in tongues"! Those who refuse or neglect the gift of tongues in their lives have a big hole in their armor that causes them to be less effective in the kingdom.

Finally, "praying in the Spirit" gives us the ability to see or watch. It is the part of the armor that puts a demand on us to watch as well as pray. Watching is a part of the armor of God. I will discuss this in depth in the next two chapters.

CHAPTER SEVEN

The Watches of the Lord (Part 1)

Being a Watchman on the Wall

I N BIBLICAL TIMES cities without walls were open for attack. Strong walls of protection were the first line of defense against the enemy's attacks. The same is true for the believer who desires to become an intercessor. In this chapter, I want to help you to know how to use basic principles of defense to build strong "prayer walls."

Nehemiah understood that restoration could not come to a city unless the walls were rebuilt. His purpose for building the walls of the city was to provide a place for the people to get back in their rightful positions—"on the wall"! Watchmen were strategically placed on the walls to sound alarms to alert the city. But before the watchmen could be assigned to their positions, strong walls had to be built.

Three things are important in building prayer walls.

1. Rule

Proverbs 25:28 says that if a person does not have rule over their own spirit, they are like a city with broken-down walls. It is important that watchmen are stable and have balance in their own lives. Every human being has issues to deal with in his or her own life. Yet intercessors who are called to be watchmen must have rule over their own spirit. They cannot be blown off the wall and overcome by every circumstance and situation. The Hebrew word for *rule* is *awtsar*, and it means:

- To fast
- To maintain
- To assemble
- To shut up
- To restrain self
- To be able to stay
- To recover

Watchmen cannot be moved out of position by the warfare that confronts them in their position. They must be able to stand firm in the midst of adverse situations. The watchmen on the wall must have self-restraint. They must also have the ability to recover in the event that they fall.

2. Structure

Walls are built to provide structure on which people may operate. A foundation gives an edifice the ability to stand and endure. Walls protect from outside elements and influences. Well-built intercessory walls provide covering for the watchmen as they pray. This prevents casualties of war during intercession.

The wall is a place where a line is drawn in the spirit. There is protection on one side and trouble on the other. The Bible teaches that it is difficult to find people to stand in the gaps or make up the hedges (Ezek. 13:5; Ps. 80:12). The word *hedge* is *gader* in Hebrew, and it refers to a wall. It is hard to find faithful people who will make up the hedges or build true prayer walls. In the Bible, walls were created with watchmen on them as an enclosure for the city. This enclosure provided a design that incorporated a plan of safety. Watchmen could be seers for the city, and at the same time the wall provided a place of safety for them.

The wall is also a place of agreement. We have too many solo soldiers and lone rangers in the body of Christ today. One intercessor can put a thousand to flight, and two, ten thousand (Deut. 32:30). Where two or more touch and agree, anything can be done (Matt. 18:19). The wall provides structure that ensures safety for all! Many attempt to stand in gaps and make up the hedges alone, and they do not endure! They suffer backlash and retaliation, which the spirit of agreement will deliver them from.

3. Assignment

Prayer assignments are very important. I have told my intercessors for years that the wall is not the place to be distracted by personal needs. A watchman must be focused on the prayer assignment. For example, if a watchman is assigned to a watch, he or she cannot get so caught up in personal worship time that the enemy slips past them and infiltrates the camp. While on duty, warfare is their worship! Paying attention to detail while standing in the gap for the entire city is urgent. The prayer assignment of the wall is not just for "me and my four and no more." When you have committed to intercession, your assignment is the cell group, auxiliary, church, or city that you are assigned to pray for.

The Bible tells us to have no thought for tomorrow for our personal needs (Matt. 6:34). If we seek God concerning the things that pertain to the kingdom, all of our needs will be taken care of (Matt. 6:33). Watchmen on the wall must be dedicated to the cause. The *spirit of need* has distracted many intercessors and become an enemy of the wall. We cannot have strong walls built by needy people. Those who know God will do great exploits. We must know Him as a provider. Only then will we know Him in power. If we cannot know Him in provision, we cannot really know Him in true power.

Being a watchman on the wall is serious business. It is not personal or recreational, but it is a life-or-death situation. Those who do not understand this can end up with blood on their hands. In Ezekiel 33, Ezekiel was the chief watchman for Israel. God told Ezekiel to tell the people to take a man from their midst and make him a watchman (v. 2). God warned Ezekiel that He was about to bring the sword (judgment) upon the land. He said that when the watchman saw the sword coming, it was the watchman's responsibility to sound the trumpet. If the watchman sounded the trumpet and the people took heed, their lives would be saved. If the watchman warned them and they did not take heed, their blood would be upon their own hands. If the watchman failed to warn the people of what he saw, the blood of the people would be on his hands.

How many in the church have neglected to say what they really saw because they did not want to offend people? I saw this manifested in the church during Hurricane Katrina. Many preachers did not want to mention the judgment of God in relationship to this storm. Months before the hurricane took place, many prophets had prophesied that New Orleans would be wiped out by water. When the storm hit, everybody acted as if God was pleased with what went on in that city. They preached that God was a God of love, and judgment was not an issue.

Someone has skipped over too many pages in the Bible; God does not play around with judgment! In Bible times, Sodom and Gomorrah were really wiped out. There are modern cities in foreign countries that have also been swallowed up because of voodoo. If America does not stop aborting babies and promoting same-sex marriages, we will understand this firsthand. Will the real watchmen in America take their rightful positions on the wall? They must say what God is saying, and forget what people think about it.

When the sword of the Lord touches the land, we must be careful not to fall under the "curse of the false watchman." Isaiah 56:10–11 talks about it:

> His watchmen are blind,
> They are all ignorant;
> They are all dumb dogs,
> They cannot bark;
> Sleeping, lying down, loving to slumber.
> Yes, they are greedy dogs
> Which never have enough.
> And they are shepherds
> Who cannot understand;
> They all look to their own way,
> Every one for his gain,
> From his own territory.

Slumber is the enemy of the wall. Too many intercessors love sleep more than they love obedience to God. Of course, we all like good sleep, but the curse comes in when sleep robs us of our anointing to watch and pray. In the military, a soldier could be put in prison for falling asleep while on an official watch. I recently prayed for a soldier in the army who lost two ranks for this same offense.

Other spirits assigned against watchmen are the spirits of greed, blindness, and ignorance. Let's study the passage on these spirits in depth.

SPIRITS ASSIGNED AGAINST WATCHMEN

Blindness

The purpose of a watchman is to be able to see. A blind watchman is useless to God.

Ignorance

To be *ignorant* means to be uninformed. Watchmen are placed on the wall to inform the people of what is happening in the spirit and how it relates to them in the natural. Watchmen have to be able to discern the times and inform the people. Religious ignorance is rampant in the church. Leaders are sometimes so superficial that they have lost touch with the supernatural. Jesus called them hypocrites! He said that they could discern the face of the sky and earth, but they were ignorant of the times. (See Luke 12:56.) This word *times* is *kairos*, and it means "set seasons, occasions, and opportunities."

The spirit of the "dumb dog" (Isa. 56:10)

The Hebrew word for *dumb* is *illem*, and it means "to bind and cause to be speechless, tongue-tied, and put to silence." The Hebrew word for *dog* is *keleb*, and means "a male prostitute; a dog that yelps (to have no bark but to sound like a dog in pain)."

This is a spirit of bondage where the person is not only bound in disobedience but also perversion and weakness. The Bible says they lie down and love to sleep. There is a Greek word for *watch* (*agrupneo*) that means "to sleep less." This person cannot sound an alarm to help anyone. He cannot even yell loud enough to help himself. When he attempts to cry out, it releases a yelp. This is a sound like a dog in pain. A good dog can sound the alarm when strangers approach. A dog that cannot bark or give an alert is useless.

When dogs are useless, they exist only to be fed and taken care of. A false watchman on the wall is only concerned about his needs being met. He does his job haphazardly with the motive of always getting something in return. This is where the term *keleb* comes into play. It is the curse of the male prostitute. All prostitution is an abomination, but male prostitution is the lowest. When a man submits his body to be sold for a price, it costs him more than he is charging. He is actually selling his headship! Prostitutes are doomed to be under the control of others and, ultimately, weak. A weak man is *ultimate weakness*! The lower a person has to stoop to do a thing, the weaker it makes them spiritually. When a man stoops to prostitution, he has to step a long way down from his place of original dominion. It is an abomination to God!

The spirit of the "greedy" dog

A watchman cannot be greedy. One of the standards listed for bishops is to abstain from all greed (1 Tim. 3:3). Proverbs 1:19 says that the spirit of greed takes away the life of the person who gains possession of the things he is greedy for. The Bible also states that if we are greedy for gain, it will bring trouble to our own homes (Prov. 15:27). There are actually people who are covetous and greedy continually all day long (Prov. 21:26). The spirit of greed opens the door to many afflictions. This spirit is a "greedy dog," which means you can add the spirit of greed to everything that I explained earlier about the male prostitute; imagine the bondage.

The spirit of "not enough"

I believe that people are bound by the spirit of "not enough" because they never sat down and counted the cost in what they pursued.

> For which of you, wishing to build a farm building, does not first sit down and calculate the cost [to see] whether he has sufficient means to finish it?
>
> —LUKE 14:28, AMP

This scripture says that people will mock your foundation if you do not have the means to finish it. They will say, "This man began to build and was not worth enough to finish it!" One of my favorite things to tell my children is, "No matter how well you start out, you have to have enough to finish." Though I am speaking on building prayer walls, this is a basic principle for life. Anything in life that is worth doing or having will cost you something. There is a price to pay in intercession! If you know that you have a prayer assignment, you must first sit down and calculate the cost. After everything has been added, subtracted, multiplied, and divided, the question must be asked: Do you have enough to finish? People are bound by the spirit of "not enough" because they did not have what they needed when they started out.

When embarking upon any assignment you must be able to ask yourself two questions:

1. Has God called you to do it?
2. Are you willing to sell out to it?

If you have this, you have enough to finish. Jesus is the author and finisher of your faith! He will watch over His word unto you to perform it. If you are not sure, wait on the Lord. Never pursue the things of God with a question mark over your head.

The spirit of self-gain (my way or no way)

Isaiah 56 ends describing spiritual leaders who looked to their own way for selfish gain. Watchmen on the wall must be careful not to fall into this same trap. They must be flexible and open to that which is not familiar to them. Familiar spirits are the enemy of the vision of the wall. Spirits that cause people to only do things their way and promote self-gain reinforce familiar spirits. It becomes a vicious cycle that is difficult to break.

CHAPTER EIGHT

The Watches of the Lord (Part 2)

What Are the Biblical Watches of the Lord?

THERE ARE DESCRIPTIONS of watches in both the Old and New Testaments. In this chapter we will discuss the various kinds of prayer watches of the Lord, but let's first take a look at the difference between an Old Testament watch and a New Testament watch.

NEW TESTAMENT WATCH

This kind of watch is when we are commanded to watch as well as pray (Luke 21:36). When the New Testament refers to this kind of watch, it speaks of watching for the return of the Lord. There are two Greek words that describe this kind of watch: *gregoreuo* and *agrupneo*. Both mean "to stay awake, be vigilant, watch, pray, and sleep less."

OLD TESTAMENT WATCH

This kind of watch is actually an assignment or duty. It relates to the watchmen on the wall who protected the city. There are two Greek words that describe this duty. *Koustodia* is related to the English word *custody*, and it means to be responsible for a watch. (See Matthew 27:65–66; 28:11.) *Phulake* means to stand guard over a person, place, or condition in a specific division or time of the day. (See Matthew 14:25; 24:43; Mark 6:48; Luke 2:8; 12:38.)

To sum it all up, the assignment of the watchman was to be the eyes and ears of the city. The attitude of a great watchman is that if anything happens, *it will not be on my watch!* The watchman should take pride in his or her duty. They should actually take custody of the watch and be liable for whatever happens. The watchman bears the burden of the responsibility of the watch and adequately covers every person, place, or thing under the jurisdiction of his watch. Jurisdiction outlines authority that is given, but it also gives the limitations. God instructed His people to set up watches that delegated authority during different shifts of the night. The Hebrew watches began when the sun went down. Even in creation, God worked from evening to morning. It is the pattern of God. In the Old Testament there were only three original watches. Each watch was four hours, and the shifts began at sundown.

THE ORIGINAL WATCHES OF THE LORD

1. The beginning watch—Lamentations 2:19

This scripture instructed the people to arise and cry out in the night at the *beginning of the watches*. This word *beginning* is *rosh* in Hebrew. It means first in time, place, and rank. It also means "most easily shaken." This is the apostolic watch that was put in place during the time that God's people considered the beginning of the day, sundown. This is why the Sabbath begins in the evening and not the morning. The people were told to pour out their hearts like water before the face of the Lord. This was the time the people lifted their hands to the Lord for the lives of their children. It was the time that darkness could be easily shaken.

In Lamentations 2:18–19 Jeremiah spoke to the *wall* as a prophetic symbol. He said, "O wall of the daughter of Zion, let tears run down like a river day and night; give yourself no relief; give your eyes no rest. Arise, cry out in the night, at the beginning of the watches." These were the cries of God's people on the first watch.

2. The middle watch—Judges 7:19

The story of Gideon in Judges 7 is often used to relate to the warfare strategy of the Lord. For our purposes I would like to relate Gideon's experience to intercession. Verses 16–19 tell how Gideon divided the three hundred men of his army into three companies. The one hundred men that were assigned to Gideon moved out in the beginning of the *middle watch* after the guards had changed. This indicates that there were indeed three watches. The word *middle* is *tiykown,* and it means "womb of the watch, or the central watch that everything else was built around." This was the watch during which evil seed was planted against the righteous. During the intercession of the watches, everything was built around this watch.

3. The morning watch—Exodus 14:24; 1 Samuel 11:11

Greek and Roman influence on the church changed things from the way God originally planned it for His people. The morning watch is considered the last watch. Our mind-sets would have us to believe that it is the first. It was during the morning watch that God discomfited the Egyptians and made their chariots drive heavy when they were chasing the Israelites into the Red Sea. As a result, the children of Israel gained victory over their enemies and escaped.

Just like Gideon, Saul divided his army into three companies, and they slew the Ammonites during the *morning watch*. It is evident that we gain victory over our enemies in the morning. This particular word *morning* is *boqer* in the Hebrew, and it refers to the breaking of day. It comes out of another Hebrew word *baqar*. This word means "to plow, break through, and seek out."

For the past ten months, my ministry team and I have been *commanding the morning* in intercession. I know what it means to seek victory in the morning by plowing through. This is the fruit of the morning watch. When you are faithful and dedicated, you can expect victory over your enemies every time.

THE NEW TESTAMENT WATCH

We know that in the New Testament, four watches are mentioned. These watches are based on the Roman clock. Because we use this as a measurement of time today, it is important that I review these watches also.

First watch: 6:00 p.m.–9:00 p.m.

This is the watch in which the sun sets. Often, they brought the sick to Jesus to be healed when the sun went down. (See Mark 1:32; Luke 4:40.) Anything that is *first* is apostolic and pioneering. This is the first watch after the morning has been commanded, and it is the time to carry out the anointing of the day. Those who gird their loins on the first watch must have the anointing to break into new territories. This is a time of miracles and the breaking of barriers. This is not the time to focus on what has been done before. The first watch is a time when those who know God will be strong and do exploits. This means to do daring and bold deeds. The first watch must start off with apostolic boldness and power.

Second watch: 9:00 p.m.–12:00 a.m.

When I think of the watches of the Lord, I think of the relay teams that I ran on in college. Just like the watches, there were four legs to the relay. Most coaches would put their best runner on the last leg, but my coach always put the best runner on the second leg. His strategy was that if he got someone who could keep us in the race on the first leg, a strong second leg runner would have us ahead in the race. A good second leg runner could control the race. It always worked! Our relay team ran the fastest times in the nation.

Using this principle, strong intercessors should be on the second watch. They should be seasoned intercessors (not beginners) who know how to move in the Spirit. We need intercessors on this watch who will give us a jump ahead of the enemy before we go into the midnight hour.

Third watch: 12:00 a.m.–3:00 a.m.

This is the watch that transitions into the darkest part of the night—midnight or the middle of the night. Witches take advantage of this deep darkness and call this period of time *the witching hour*. Despite their efforts, all the watches belong to the Lord! This is a time that witches take pleasure in planting seeds of witchcraft. They have attempted to hijack this watch, which God has created for us. At this time we need intercessors who are not afraid to overturn the false rule of witches. We need intercessors who will intercede and take back from the enemy the authority that he has attempted to steal. It will require disciplined, stable intercessors who are not afraid to deal with witchcraft on this watch. I would not put novices on this watch.

Fourth watch: 3:00 a.m.–6:00 a.m.

This is the watch of the early risers and commanders of the morning. The activities of the day are established during this watch. During this time we hijack the airways of the morning to declare the prosperity of our days. It was on the fourth watch when Jesus walked on the water. (See Matthew 14:25–33.) Chapter ten in this book, on becoming a commander of the morning, will give you more information about this fourth watch. (People who are new to intercession or who have never been on a wall should be placed on the first or fourth watch.)

In the last days, God is placing a mandate on His church to wake up, to watch and pray. Matthew 24:43 tells us, "If the master of the house had known what hour the thief would come, he would have watched and not allowed his house to be broken into." The word *thief* is *kleptes,* and it is related to the word *kleptomaniac.* A kleptomaniac is someone who steals by nature and without a cause. Satan is a natural thief! You do not have to do anything but live, and if he has not tried to rob you, he will. He is a kleptomaniac. The master of the house in this verse was a good man who got robbed. Most people think that the devil attacks people who have done something wrong. No, he attacks good men! The man's house was broken into. The word *broken* is *diorusso,* and it means that his security was penetrated and his house undermined. When something is undermined, it means that the foundation was secretly weakened.

I believe that many of the tragic events that we have experienced recently in America are causing the watchmen to be stirred to get back on the walls. The thief has penetrated our security, and it is causing us to raise the standard of security. Just as the government is raising the standard of natural security, the saints are raising the standard of supernatural security. They are getting back on the walls and securing the night watches.

Isaiah 52:8 speaks of watchmen who will see eye to eye. Isaiah 21:6 says that we must set watchmen on the walls who will not be afraid to declare what they see. I prophesy these scriptures over America! Our watchmen will see eye to eye, and they will be bold to declare what they see!

Let's review the scriptures on this topic:

> Prepare the table,
> Set a watchman in the tower,
> Eat and drink.

Arise, you princes,
Anoint the shield!

For thus has the Lord said to me:
"Go, set a watchman,
Let him declare what he sees."

—ISAIAH 21:5–6

Then he cried, "A lion, my Lord!
I stand continually on the watchtower in the daytime;
I have sat at my post every night."

—ISAIAH 21:8

The watchtower was an observatory set up for military purposes. This is where the sentries set up their post. The churches in America are setting up watchtowers that will be observatories. The cries of the watchmen will sound alarms that will not only affect our country, but will also set new standards for building prayer walls worldwide.

THE DIFFERENCE BETWEEN WATCHMEN AND GATEKEEPERS

In Nehemiah 7, we learn that the wall was completed. After the completion of the building of the wall, people were placed in strategic positions on it (v. 3). They also had porters (v. 45, KJV). This word *porter* is *shoer*, and it means to act as a gatekeeper.

The question came to my mind: What is the difference between a gatekeeper and a watchman? The first thing that I would like to note is that a person cannot be on the wall and effectively control the traffic of the gates at the same time. They are two completely different functions. To illustrate this truth, let's look at the issue of airport security in America. Security guards are stationed at the gates of the front part of the terminal. Only passengers or employees of the airport can go through these gates. The gates are checkpoints to the areas of the airport with higher security.

Two things are generally checked at these points: credentials and contraband. The guards at these gates are not usually armed, but they have the authority to allow entrance. There are also armed officials, strategically stationed around the airport, who are generally out of sight. They are secret agents and U.S. marshals who are heavily armed, yet they wander around unnoticed. They have the true firepower behind the scenes. You never know who these people are until trouble comes.

When a problem arises, they jump out of nowhere to deal with the situation. The *gatekeeper* is the person on terminal security, and the *watchman* is the U.S. marshal behind the scenes. Everyone knows who the gatekeepers of cities are, but watchmen on the walls hold the firepower behind the scenes. Though gatekeepers walk in great authority, the true power of intercession, that of the watchman, is behind the scenes.

Gatekeepers control the flow of traffic in a city; they allow the *right ones* to enter. On the other hand, the watchman on the wall has a strong discernment for the enemy. The more experienced the watchman is, the further away he or she can detect the approach of the enemy. It is very difficult to check for the right ones and to keep your eyes on the enemy off in the distance at the same time. Though all intercessors must have a defensive and offensive disposition, gatekeepers and watchmen maintain different general functions of intercession.

In 1 Chronicles 9 they ordained and set into office two hundred twelve gatekeepers (v. 22). They also ordained four chief gatekeepers who were watchmen and gatekeepers (v. 26). This proves that one person can do both functions, but it is a rare position. In this position they had two assignments:

1. They had the responsibility of manning the watch.
2. They opened the house every morning (keeping the gates).

Recently I had what I know to be a prophetic dream. I was fighting witches with a powerful sword. I was cutting them up with this sword. They were outside of the house at first, but later penetrated the house and got inside. I turned to a lady in my ministry and yelled for her to go and let everyone know that witches were in the house. When I looked into her eyes, somehow I all of a sudden knew that she was a plant from the other side. She realized that her cover was blown, and she ran off.

I immediately ran up a stairway, and a loud alarm was going off. It sounded like an alarm on a navy ship. I was knocking on doors and yelling, "Wake up; witches are in the house!" People in my leadership were sleeping in their rooms, and they began to come out to see what was going on. Though we all lived at different addresses, when this alarm sounded, we all had a room in the same house. This is how it is in the spirit. In the body of Christ, when the enemy attacks the church, we all have a room in it. In the dream our gates were penetrated by witches, and they infiltrated the house. We need watchmen in our churches today who will sound the alarm concerning enemy infiltration. The chief gatekeepers closed the gates at night and opened them in the morning.

Earlier I noted the significance of the gatekeepers and the watchmen. There are exceptions to the rule. When it comes to spiritual warfare, my favorite rule is that "there are no rules."

> And Zechariah the son of Meshelemiah was porter of the door of the tabernacle of the congregation. All these which were chosen to be porters in the gates were two hundred and twelve. These were reckoned by their genealogy in their villages, whom David and Samuel the seer did ordain in their set office. So they and their children had the oversight of the gates of the house of the Lord, namely, the house of the tabernacle, by wards [watches].
>
> In four quarters were the porters, toward the east, west, north, and south. And their brethren, which were in their villages, were to come after seven days from time to time with

them. For these Levites, the four chief porters, were in their set office, and were over the chambers and treasuries of the house of God. And they lodged round about the house of God, because the charge was upon them, and the opening thereof every morning pertained to them.

—1 Chronicles 9:21–27, KJV

The chief porters (gatekeepers) were not only in charge of the traffic of the gates every morning, but they also had a "charge" upon them. The word *charge* is *mishmereth,* and it means to be a sentry on a post stationed for a watch. I think it is interesting to note that the porters involved their children in the oversight of the gates of the house of the Lord. The assignment of the enemy is to kill our seed. It is pertinent that we train our young people in high-level intercession. Young people in America are taking on major issues in America in our justice system. This is a good thing! There are things that go on in darkness that the next generation will bring to the light.

CHAPTER NINE

The Night Watches

Satan's Counterfeit Watch

Though the watches of the Lord begin at sunset and continue throughout sunrise, this is a different kind watch of "night watch." It is referring to the demonic night watches. The psalmist said that he *prevented* or anticipated them.

> I prevented the dawning of the morning, and cried: I hoped in thy word. Mine eyes prevent the night watches, that I might meditate in thy word.
>
> —Psalm 119:147–148, KJV

Throughout this book, I have reminded you of a very important principle in warfare: everything that God has, the devil counterfeits.

The devil has a counterfeit night watch. The word *night* in Psalm 119:148 was inserted by translators; it refers back to the usage of *night* in Genesis 1:5. In the Hebrew language the word *night* is *layil,* and it means "adversity that comes in darkness or that which is far away from the light." Many are afraid to admit it, but there are things that go bump in the night.

Psalm 91:5 promises protection from the terror that comes by night. This word *night* is also *layil*. Therefore, the Book of Psalms confirms the fact that there are things that go on in the night from which we need to be protected. If you cannot pick up what I am saying in the spirit, let's take a look at some natural circumstances. Have you noticed that when a person has a sickness or cold, the symptoms get worse at night? When daylight breaks, the symptoms seem to get better.

In Nehemiah 7:3 the gatekeepers were warned to keep the gates closed until the sun got hot. This literally meant that the gates of Jerusalem were to stay closed until the ministry of the sun reached its greatest potential. The word *sun* is *shemash,* and it means "daylight activity or ministry." Every part of the heavens has a ministry or an assignment given by God.

The Bible also tells us how weeping may endure at night, but joy comes in the morning (Ps. 30:5). When Jacob was wrestling with the angel, he held on to the angel until the breaking of day (Gen. 32:24). The word *breaking* is *àlah,* and it means "to make to rise up or to lift self up." This word also means "to restore or recover." Yes, it is true. There is help that comes in the morning. This is when God steps in to deliver us from the assignments (seeds) of the enemy that have been planted at night. I minister to many witches and warlocks who attempt to transition to the Lord's side. They all say the same thing: evil is at its highest point during the darkest hours of the night. The high point starts at midnight or in the middle of the night when light is furthest away from the earth.

People from the dark side have attempted to hijack this time of the night and label it the "witching hour." It is generally from 12:00 a.m. to 3:00 a.m. I have news for the devil and his crew... *every minute of the day belongs to the Lord.* Psalm 74:16 says that the day and the night belong to the Lord. Unfortunately, the devil is stupid enough to think otherwise. He continues to release terrors that come by night. Many people are attacked in the wee hours of the night in their dream lives, and they pay it no attention. Dreams are very real! As a matter of fact, my dreams are sometimes more real to me than when I wake up. I am a dreamer, and I actually get caught between realms at times when I am sleeping and can see clear plans of the enemy.

On one occasion after I was first saved, I saw a skull go down my throat while I was sleeping. As I was sleeping, it seemed to only be a dream, but the reality was that I was awakened with congestion in my chest that did not leave for many years. I was in Japan the week that the airborne disease SARS broke out. I was baffled as to why everyone was wearing face masks. I did not find out what was really going on until I left Japan and went to Hong Kong. One night while I was sleeping in Hong Kong, a demon attacked me in my physical body. It seemed to be going down my throat. As I slept, I felt my throat burning, and my body was very weak. I felt like I was dying! The demon spoke to me in my sleep and announced that he was the demon from the outbreak of sickness in Japan. It did not have a name at the time. I literally wrestled with this demon all night. He was telling me that I was going to die, and I was telling him that when I got up in the morning I would be totally healed.

The next morning I was healed, but the soreness from the demon going down my throat was still there. God allowed me to know that I was not just dreaming. I had had an encounter with the death spirit SARS. My sponsors in Hong Kong sent a local doctor to my room. He confirmed that I was fine. The next night I warned the people of Hong Kong that the disease that was loosed in Japan had come to Hong Kong. No one paid much attention to what I said at the time. The disease did not do much damage in Japan, but later that year it was on the news worldwide that the epidemic killed a large number of people in Hong Kong. The words that I spoke did not fall to the ground. This disease was a terror that came by night. It was a literal spirit of death.

I believe that even the tactics of terrorism are heightened at night. The plans and seeds are planted so that arrows will be released in the day. I was commanding the morning recently, and God woke me up and gave me a certain word. I do not feel led to release that word at this time. I looked the word up on the Internet, and when I pressed the key I was immediately taken to a terrorist Web site. I alerted my intercessors, and we began to do warfare against terrorist attacks. Within a few days of this incident a terrorist group was dismantled in Miami, Florida. They were meeting in an old warehouse in a poor neighborhood, and they were training at night. Just as the psalmist declared, "we prevented the night watches."

This word *prevented* means "to anticipate." God will give us the ability to anticipate the plans of our enemies. In 2 Kings 6:12, God showed Elisha the things that the king of Syria spoke in his bedchamber against the king of Israel. This prevented Israel from being attacked, because they were warned of the enemy's plans. What a powerful move of God! We should expect God to keep us three steps ahead of our enemy.

I have a rap song called, "Devil, Boo, I See You!" This refers to when the enemy is hiding around the corner waiting to startle us. We are living in the day when the saints will peep around the corner and tell the devil, "It won't work—I saw you coming!" The only power of the spirit of terror is in the fact that it catches us off guard.

THE SECRET COUNSEL OF THE WICKED

In the sixty-fourth chapter of Psalms, David prayed a prayer for aid against his enemies. This scripture has comforted so many who come under the demonic attack of night watches. You will not understand what I am talking about unless you have experienced this kind of attack.

If you have been experiencing warfare, you need to understand that you have been under the attack of the *demonic night watches*. God says that His people perish for a lack of knowledge (Hosea 4:6). Witches and warlocks take advantage of Christians who do not believe that these things exist.

David was a man after God's own heart, but even he prayed for relief from the demonic night watches:

Hear my voice, O God, in my meditation;
Preserve my life from fear [terror] of the enemy.
Hide me from the secret plots of the wicked,
From the rebellion of the workers of iniquity,
Who sharpen their tongue like a sword,
And bend their bows to shoot their arrows—bitter words,
That they may shoot in secret at the blameless;
Suddenly they shoot at him and do not fear.

They encourage themselves in an evil manner;
They talk of laying snares secretly;
They say, "Who will see them?"
They devise iniquities:
"We have perfected a shrewd scheme."
Both the inward thought and the heart of man are deep.

But God shall shoot at them with an [unexpected] arrow;
Suddenly they shall be wounded.
So He will make them stumble over their own tongue;
All who see them shall flee away.
All men shall fear,
And shall declare the work of God;
For they shall wisely consider His doing.

The righteous shall be glad in the LORD, and trust in Him.
And all the upright in heart shall glory.
—PSALM 64:1–10

It is so difficult for believers to understand that there are people on the other side who do not play fair. They intentionally want to destroy us. In Psalm 119:161, David spoke of princes who pursued and persecuted him without a cause.

You may be thinking, *I have not done anything to anybody*. Well, the truth of the matter is that you still qualify to be under the attack of the night watches. Scripture says that they shoot arrows at the blameless. The King James Version uses the word *perfect.* This word, *perfect,* means "the just or upright." They love to attack the innocent.

The Hebrew word *layil,* translated *night* in Psalm 119:148, is directly related to another word, *Lilith.* Lilith is the demon of the desert mentioned in the Old Testament. She is known as the screech owl or night hag in Isaiah 34:14. In the Babylonian language this spirit is known as *Lamashtu.* Lilith is the symbol of the women's feminist movement, and they have Lilith Festivals around America in tribute to this demon.

Lilith is a man-hating spirit. In folklore she is an avowed enemy of God. This demon vows to kill all babies before they reach the age of one. When I pray against crib death, I bind the spirit of Lilith. It is a nightmare spirit that suffocates babies in their sleep.

Incubus and Succubus spirits are also nightmares. A nightmare is not just a dream. It is an attack by a spirit. Nightmares can occur in the daytime or at night. The hour in which these spirits attack is not what is significant. It is their presence that promotes terror while one is sleeping at any time of the day. A *nightmare* is defined as a dream that is accompanied by oppression and helplessness. Whenever oppression is a manifestation, the devil is operating behind the scenes.

Many famous people have mysteriously died in their sleep. It is no mystery to me. Though medical professionals have given a natural diagnosis, I believe that that source of the problem is spiritual. They are manifestations of night terrors.

The enemy extends his power by privately and secretly laying down snares for believers. Jude 4 talks about "certain men" who crept into the church "unawares." This word is *pareisduno,* which means "to infiltrate and grow up alongside." Moses grew up alongside the Pharaohs, and his knowledge of them from the inside eventually worked against them. Judas worked by Jesus' side. The closer the attacker can get to his target, the more successful his attempts will be. Jesus anticipated Judas's motives. He eventually released Judas to do what he had determined to do (John 13:27). Judas merely helped Jesus to accomplish His overall mission. Sometimes God will even allow enemies to get in close to us so that we can fulfill His call on our lives.

The wicked take pride in saying, "Who shall see us?" (Ps. 64:5). But their efforts are futile when we have anticipated what they will attempt during the night watches. When we rise early to command our mornings, the Bible says that our prayers go forth and meet God—and our enemies are scattered.

> Let God arise,
> Let His enemies be scattered;
> Let those also who hate Him flee before Him.
>
> —PSALM 68:1

> But to You I cry, O Lord; and in the morning shall my prayer come to meet You.
>
> —PSALM 88:13, AMP

Because we love the Lord, it may be difficult to understand that there are people who hate God. But if they hate God, and you love the Lord, THEY HATE YOU! People who do not like me do not take kindly to my children. Wicked men hate you because you are a child of God. Jesus warns us that if the world hated Him, they will hate us also (John 15:18).

There are, however, repercussions for those who hate God and His children. Psalm 64:7 speaks of how God will shoot an unexpected arrow at those who lay snares and shoot secret arrows at His children. They attacked suddenly, and they will receive the vengeance of God suddenly. They will be wounded, and their own tongues will become weapons against them (vv. 7–8). God will turn the words that they spoke against you against them! And all men will see what God will do to them. Because of God's vengeance, they will not be able to give any glory to the devil for his secret plots. Instead, all men will "wisely consider" what God is doing.

Who are the people who man the night watches? They are the ones who rebel against the light. Job 24:13 says that they do not know the way of the light or how to stay in its path:

> These wrongdoers are of *those who rebel against the light*; they know not its ways nor stay in its paths. The murderer rises with the light; he kills the poor and the needy, and in the night he becomes a thief. The eye also of the adulterer waits for the twilight, saying, No eye shall see me, and he puts a disguise upon his face. In the dark, they dig through [the penetrable walls of] houses; by day they shut themselves up; they do not know the sunlight. For midnight is morning to all of them; for they are familiar with the terrors of deep darkness.
> —JOB 24:13–17, AMP, EMPHASIS ADDED

This scripture warns us that when it gets dark, evil men attempt to penetrate our walls of protection. We are children of the light, and light always takes out darkness. Though weapons form against us in the midnight hour, God will keep us through the night. Our enemies are defeated by the break of day.

THE ANOINTING OF THE TWILIGHT

Twilight means to be in a place of transition or neutrality. It also means to be in a place where things are not clearly defined. The prefix *twi* means "two," so we are safe in saying that *twilight* means to be between two lights.

> And God said, Let there be lights in the expanse of the heavens to separate the day from the night, and let them be signs and tokens [of God's provident care], and [to mark] seasons, days, and years, and let them be lights in the expanse of the sky to give light upon the earth. And it was so. And God made the two great lights—the greater light (the sun) to rule the day and the lesser light (the moon) to rule the night. He also made the stars.
> —GENESIS 1:14–16, AMP

God created two great lights. When these lights change shifts—either from daytime to sunset or from nighttime to sunrise—it is called *twilight*. The key word is *shift*. During twilight, time literally changes from one shift to the other. As I searched the Scriptures concerning the twilight, I discovered that many significant things occurred during this time of day.

We can draw from the anointed revelations about the twilight hour. First Samuel 30:17 says that David smote the Philistines during the twilight. Second Kings 7:5 tells the story of the lepers who got up at twilight during the famine in Samaria. They left the gate of Samaria at twilight to go to the enemy camp of the Syrians. They discovered that their enemies were simultaneously fleeing (at twilight) out of the Syrian camp because they heard the "noise of a great army" (v. 7). In their haste to flee, the Syrians left their spoils for the lepers to enjoy when they got there. The lepers obeyed God even though things were not clear to them. The twilight hour is a time of obedience. It is when you stand between the challenge and the breakthrough. In Hebrew, the word *twilight* is *nehsef,* and it means:

- "Beginning of light"
- "Moving toward light"
- "Growing light"
- "That which is developing or which
  one is beginning to perceive"

The lepers knew that they could not stay where they were. They had no choice but to move toward the promise (light). Even in a place of obscurity, we must purpose to move toward the promise. The promise is represented by the light. This is why evil men do not know the way of the light. They have no hope or promise in God.

The first step in moving toward a thing is getting up. The lepers had to first "get up" before they could "move forward." Do not be discouraged if you have been knocked down in battle. The Bible encourages us that a righteous man will fall down seven times and rise up again, but the wicked shall fall into mischief (Prov. 24:16). The lepers rose again! In their risen state, God prompted them to not forget where they had come from. He demanded that they share the spoils with the Israelite city. The same light that blessed them would be a curse to them if they did not do right.

> Then they said one to another, We are not doing right. This is a day of [glad] good news and we are silent and do not speak up! If we wait until daylight, some punishment will come upon us [for not reporting at once]. So now come, let us go and tell the king's household.
>
> —2 KINGS 7:9, AMP

The twilight demands obedience. Ephesians 4:26 warns us not to let the sun go down on our wrath. When we are obedient to God, we get in place to have victory over the wicked. The devil can counterfeit everything except obedience to God! It gives us the upper hand against darkness.

Malachi 4:2–3 assures us that if we fear the name of the Lord, the Sun of Righteousness shall rise up on our behalf with healing in His wings. As a result of this, we shall tread down the wicked, and they shall become ashes under the soles of our feet. Psalm 101:8 also adds that morning after morning we can uproot wickedness from the land so that evildoers will be eliminated from the city of the Lord. This is the fuel that was put in my tank to become a commander of the morning during the fourth watch. You can learn more about this watch in the next chapter.

Chapter Ten

Enlisting to Become a Commander of the Morning

What Is a Commander of the Morning?

Aᴌᴌ ᴏꜰ ᴍʏ life I had never been a morning person. Then at the beginning of my salvation, the Lord started awakening me in the wee hours of the morning. I have always enjoyed worshiping, studying the Word, and spending time with God in the morning. There is just something special about it. Recently I have become a commander of the morning, and it has changed my life! To understand what I mean by becoming a "commander of the morning," I must walk you through the Word of God.

> Have you commanded the morning since your days began,
> And caused the dawn to know its place,
> That it [light] might take hold of the ends of the earth,
> And the wicked [those of the night] be shaken out of it?
> —Jᴏʙ 38:12–13

It is clear that God was painting the picture to Job of who He is...the Creator. Though this was a rebuke to Job, it should become fuel in the tank of an End-Time believer. God reminded Job that he had not commanded the morning or caused the dawn to know its place so that wickedness could be shaken out of the heavens.

The position that I would like to take on this matter is that what Job did not do, we can! Jesus defeated darkness and gave the keys of the kingdom of heaven to every believer. These keys can unlock doors in the spirit to capturing our days! With them we can use the life and death of our tongues to decree the will of God for our lives.

When God created mankind, He gave us dominion over the things of the air, the sea, and on the earth. The scary part is that He did not give dominion to Christians (they did not exist at the time); He gave it to mankind! Witches and warlocks have been walking in this dominion for years, while the church has religiously sat back and accepted anything that was dealt out to them in life.

We do not have to accept things as the enemy would lay them out in life. We can unlock the will of God in the heavens. First, it is important to know that there are demonic checkpoints in the heavens. These checkpoints have been used to manipulate our days. Wicked men have tapped into the supernatural to attempt to control our destinies. Those who command their mornings can capture their days. Every wicked plan that the enemy has planted can be shaken out of the heavens to manifest victory on earth.

I realize that this teaching is not common or comfortable. As I take you through the Scriptures, I pray that you will arise and shine in the light of this revelation. We are living in the last days, and the times are not getting easier. God is activating a generation of early risers so that we can deprogram the plans of the enemy for our days. In doing this, we can also reprogram our days for the will of God.

God spoke to me clearly and said that He would give me mysteries to bring heaven down to earth. Many people are trying to get to heaven, and this is a good thing. I want to go to heaven, but I also want more out of life on earth. To get more out of life, we must pray prayers that bring heaven down to earth. Jesus told us that we should pray that the kingdom would come so that the will of God would be done in earth just as it is in heaven (Matt. 6:10).

When we hijack the airways of the morning watch, heaven comes down to earth. I mentioned the fourth watch in the last chapter. I do not think it is coincidental that Jesus walked on the water during the fourth watch. I relate the fourth watch to the fourth quarter of a game. It does not matter what has taken place in the first three quarters (watches). Anything can happen in the fourth watch.

The Bible speaks of enemies who devise wickedness against the innocent at night (Micah 2:1). Psalm 91:5 speaks of the terror of the night. At 6:00 p.m. the days start moving toward darkness, and wicked people start lurking. We used to have a saying in the world, "The freaks come out at night." Oh, how true this is! This is why many people cannot sleep; the tormentors are released at night.

As I mentioned in the last chapter, many sicknesses and curses are demonically transferred in the night hours. God's answer to the terror of the night is a radical force of commanders that will rise early in the morning to reverse the curses of the night. This will be done through early praise and worship, intercession, declarations, and decrees.

The intercessors who rise early for prayer duty must have a revelation of dominion. This dominion is basically the authority God has given us over everything He created. We have dominion in our tongues to speak to things. Jesus told the disciples that they could have a level of authority to speak to mountains, and the mountains would be removed (Matt. 21:21). The Bible also says that we can speak things that are not as though they were (Rom. 4:17).

Based on this, I can safely say that we can speak to things, and we can also speak things into existence. When Proverbs 18:21 speaks of the power of the tongue, it is actually referring to the dominion of the tongue. There is dominion in the tongue that can shift nations.

Men operated in this kind of dominion throughout the Bible. Elijah commanded the heavens to close and not rain for over three years, and they obeyed (James 5:17). Joshua spoke to the sun and the moon and commanded them to stand still, and it was so (Josh. 10:12). Where is this kind of dominion in the church today?

America is the modern-day "land of milk and honey." Our Western mind-set has stunted true dominion in our churches, and it has had a great impact on us spiritually. We have become comfortable and content while the churches in other countries have no choice but to walk in the untapped power of God. In America, we have too many options! We must be careful not to prosper to the point of becoming powerless. This chapter is my testimony of how we can walk in the dominion that God has reserved for the last days. Jesus commanded us to do "greater works" than He did!

This chapter will confirm the fact that we can obey Him in this realm today. I see it and experience it all the time! Recently, I was in Montgomery, Alabama, at a meeting. I stopped at a bookstore to get some books. The parking lot of the bookstore was filled with small black birds. They were flying about fifteen feet above the parking lot. They filled the trees, and there were so many on the phone lines I thought they would break. Everyone was acting as though this was normal. I sensed that it was not normal. I knew something was wrong.

When I asked my driver about it, he responded by indicating it was nothing. I quietly put my hands on the window of the limo (no one in the car could hear me) and said very softly, "If this is witchcraft, go, in Jesus' name!" What I immediately saw blew my mind. There had to have been one hundred thousand birds congregated over that parking lot. As I spoke, every bird lifted up in the air in lines (like smoke) and disappeared into the sky like dots. There was not one bird left.

The ironic thing is that I was not entirely serious when I spoke. I thought, *Wow, that's really speaking to the mountain!* Everyone in the car witnessed the birds leaving, but they did not hear my words. The birds did not scatter; they went up into the sky in a pattern. As the people who were traveling with me wondered aloud about what had happened, I explained to them what I had said, and we all drove away with our mouths wide open.

From this incident, I really received a revelation of the power of the tongue. There is life and death in the power of the tongue! Even though I was joking around, it did not take the power from my words.

As I thought about what had happened, I remembered what a great man of God, Dr. Kingsley Fletcher, had once told me: "Everything God created has ears." Though I whispered from far off in the seclusion of my car, the birds heard and obeyed.

I agree that all things have ears. If this were not true, the things that God created would not have heard Him when He spoke them into existence. At Creation, God spoke to things that were not, and they heard Him and began to exist.

In the church, we say that *El Shaddai* means "the God of more than enough." I was once talking to a Hebrew scribe who said that this was not the correct interpretation for *El Shaddai*. He said that it means "the God who said, 'Enough!'" He explained that if God had not said enough, things would have continued to be created. When God speaks, all of creation is attentive. Today, we have that same authority.

Did you know that the morning has ears? Every day all of creation awaits the manifestation of the true sons of God. Who are they? They are the ones who will walk in dominion over everything that God created. God created us to have dominion over everything He created, and He has placed all creation under our feet. We must walk in His dominion.

Not only does the morning have ears, but it also has a womb and wings. As the sons of God, we can speak spermatic words that will impregnate the morning. When the sun breaks out in the day, it will give birth to the will of God for our days. Do not be afraid to deal in the heavens. The heavens were created to speak on our behalf. The heavens were created to declare God's glory, and our destinies are a part of that glory. If I were you, I would delight in coming into agreement with the heavens to declare what God has for me and to put my enemies to open shame.

Psalm 119:147 says that we can anticipate the dawning of the morning and our eyes can prevent the night watches of evil watchmen. Will you get up in the morning and blind the third eye of the enemy that watches over your destiny? Will you become a fourth-watch sentry? At the end of this chapter there is a prayer and some Scripture references to get you started on your way.

We have over six thousand intercessors signed up on my Web site to command the morning. We have two thousand intercessors in Costa Rica who are currently commanding the morning also. Joy Strang, director of finance for *Charisma* magazine and wife of Stephen Strang, founder and publisher of the magazine, has thirty-five hundred intercessors who have joined us in prayer. To sum it up, almost twelve thousand people are praying over issues that concern our everyday lives, and we have witnessed miraculous moves of God.

God gave us the assignment to pray against the hurricanes. We declared in May 2006 that we would not have a hurricane season. As of this date, America has not experienced one hurricane! I believe the results of our efforts are not a secret. When there is really agreement in prayer, God moves! When we pray the will of God, He moves! Whatever we say really happens! When we told the storms to go northeast, they went northeast. When we commanded the storms to be depressed, the weather men announced that they hit land and became tropical depressions. The weather men predicted that 2006 would be the worst storm season ever. We prophesied against their words on the fourth watch, and their words were turned. They stood before the world confused! Just as God said He would do in 1 Corinthians 1:19, He baffled the minds of the logicians and the statisticians. In obedience to His Word, we shut the mouths of the prognosticators. At first the professionals said there would be eleven major storms in the Atlantic, then they changed it to seven. Now they are down to five. I say there will be zero! God's wants the world to know that He is still in charge, and He is using His powerful bride to prove it.

Since we have started commanding our mornings and capturing our days, we have seen God move in the political arenas, professional athletics, and even in Hollywood. The testimony that I take to heart is the fact that my son Michael was just placed on the roster for the

New York Giants. He did not just make the team, but God is sending his name before him. He has offers for major endorsement contracts, and HBO is currently putting together a documentary about his story and mine. People cannot believe that he really made a NFL team with no college experience. Though he has been cut five times, time worked on his behalf. The day he made the team, a movie was released called *Invincible*. This is the story of a man that made the Philadelphia Eagles team with no experience. I believe that it was a prophetic sign. When we decree and declare that which seems impossible to man, God will back it up with signs and wonders.

To sign up for my prayer force and become a commander of the morning, you may log in at www.kimberlydaniels.com.

THE "COMMANDER OF THE MORNING" PRAYER

Father God, in the name of Jesus, I rise early to declare Your lordship! I get under the covering and anointing of the early riser. I come in agreement with the heavens to declare Your glory. Lord, release the mysteries unto me to bring heaven down to earth. The stars (chief angels) are battling on my behalf ahead of time.

My appointed times have been set by God in the heavens. I declare spermatic words that will make contact with the womb of the morning and make her pregnant. At sunrise the dawn will give birth to the will of God, and light will shine on wickedness to shake it from the heavens. At twilight my enemies will flee, and newly found spoils will await me at my destination. My destiny is inevitable!

O God, let my prayers meet You this morning. I command the morning to open its ears unto me and hear my cry. Let conception take place so that prayer will rain down and be dispatched upon the earth to do Your will.

I command the earth to get in place to receive heavenly instructions on my behalf. My lands are subdued. I command all the elements of creation to take heed and obey. As my praise resounds and the day breaks, the earth shall yield her increase unto me. I declare that the first light has come!

The first fruit of my morning is holy, and the entire day will be holy. I prophesy the will of God to the morning so that the dayspring (dawn) will know its place in my days. I decree that the first light will shake wickedness from the four corners of the earth. The lines (my portion) are fallen on my behalf in pleasant (sweet, agreeable) places, and I have a secure heritage.

I am strategically lined up with the ladder that touches the third heaven and sits on earth. The angels are descending and ascending according to the words that I speak. Whatever I bind or loose on earth is already bound or loosed in heaven. Revelation, healing, deliverance, salvation, peace, joy, relationships, finances, and resources that have been demonically blocked are being loosed unto me now! What is being released unto me is transferring to every person that I associate myself with. I am contagiously blessed!

As I command the morning and capture the day, time is being redeemed. The people of God have taken authority over the fourth watch of the day. The spiritual airways and highways are being hijacked for Jesus. The atmosphere of the airways over me, my family, my church, my community, my city, my state, my nation, and the world is producing a new climate. This new climate is constructing a godly stronghold in times of trouble. The thinking of people will be conducive to the agenda of the kingdom of heaven.

Every demonic agenda or evil thought pattern designed against the agenda of the kingdom of heaven is destroyed at the root of conception, in Jesus' name! I come into agreement with the saints—as we have suffered violence, we take by force! No longer will we accept anything demonic that is dealt unto us in our days. I declare that the kingdom has come, and the will of God will be done on earth as it is in heaven.

As the sun rises today, let it shine favorably upon the people and the purposes of God. Daily destiny is my portion because I have no thought for tomorrow. I am riding on the wings of the morning into a new day of victory. God, You separated the night and the day to declare my days, years, and seasons. I am the light of the earth, and I have been separated from darkness. This light declares my destiny!

The Lord has given me dominion over the elements and all the work of His hands. He has placed them under my feet. Because I fear the name of the Lord, the Sun of Righteousness shall arise with healing in His wings, and I shall tread down the wicked until they become ashes under my feet. I commit to walk in this dominion daily. I decree and declare a new day, a new season, and a fresh anointing. As the ordinances of the constellations have received orders from God on my behalf, they shall manifest in the earth realm. The ingredients of my destiny are programmed into my days, years, and seasons. I bind every force that would attempt to capture my destiny illegitimately.

I plead the blood of Jesus over every principality, power, ruler of darkness, and spiritual wickedness in high places assigned against my purpose. I bind every destiny pirate, destiny thief, and destiny devourer in the name of Jesus! They are dethroned and dismantled and have no influence over my days. Every curse sent against my days is reversed and boomeranged back to the pits of hell. I displace the Luciferian spirit.

I bind every false light-bearer and counterfeit son of the morning. My prayers will disrupt dark plans and give my enemies a nonprosperous day. I have victory over my enemies every morning. Because I obey the Lord and serve Him, my days will prosper! This is the day that the Lord has made, and I will rejoice and be glad in it! Amen.

When you pray this prayer:

1. Start out by reading this prayer verbatim.

2. When you have researched the Scriptures and have an understanding of what you are praying, begin to ad lib and expound with your own words as you read through the prayer. (See Scripture references below.)

3. Have your prayer targets listed before you pray. Create your own, but please agree with us on the prayer points that will be given to the Commander of the Morning on a weekly basis.

4. Be prepared for prophetic insight from God as you pray, and make a listing to use in your prayer time. (Have pen and paper available.)

5. Contact us at morningcommander@kimberlydaniels .com for testimonies, revelations, and comments.

SCRIPTURE REFERENCES
(FOR COMMANDER OF THE MORNING PRAYER)

The heavens declare the glory of God.

—PSALM 19:1

They [Deborah and Barak] fought from the heavens;
The stars [princes] from their courses [heavenly pathways]
    fought against Sisera.

—JUDGES 5:20

Your people shall be volunteers
In the day of Your power;
In the beauties of holiness, from the womb of the morning.

—PSALM 110:3

Have you commanded the morning since your days began,
And caused the dawn to know its place,
That it might take hold of the ends of the earth,
And the wicked be shaken out of it?

—JOB 38:12–13

They [the lepers] rose at twilight [the light between night and sunrise] to go to the camp of the Syrians; . . . Therefore they [the Syrians] arose and fled at twilight, and left the camp intact—their tents, their horses, and their donkeys [and all their spoils]—and they fled for their lives.

—2 KING 7:5, 7

But to You I have cried out, O LORD,
And in the morning my prayer comes before You.

—PSALM 88:13

Let the peoples praise You, O God;
Let all the peoples praise You.
Then the earth shall yield her increase;
God, our own God, shall bless us.

PSALM 67:5–6

Now the whole congregation of the children of Israel assembled together at Shiloh, and set up the tabernacle of meeting there. And the land was subdued before them.

—JOSHUA 18:1

The lines [inheritance or lot in life] have fallen to me in pleas-
    ant [sweet, agreeable] places;
Yes, I have a good [legitimate and conforming to the estab-
    lished rules that God has laid out for me in the heavens]
    inheritance.

—PSALM 16:6

Then he [Jacob] dreamed, and behold, a ladder was set up on the earth, and its top reached to [the third] heaven; and there the angels of God were ascending and descending on it.

—GENESIS 28:12

And I will give you the keys of the kingdom of heaven, and whatever you bind on earth will be bound in heaven, and whatever you loose on earth will be loosed in heaven.

—MATTHEW 16:19

Now it was told King David, saying, "The LORD has blessed the house of Obed-Edom and all that belongs to him [he was contagiously blessed]."

—2 SAMUEL 6:12

But the prince of the kingdom of Persia withstood me [blocked Daniel's blessing] twenty-one days; and behold, Michael, one of the chief princes [angels] came to help me.

—DANIEL 10:13

See then that you walk circumspectly, not as fools but as wise, redeeming the time, because the days are evil.

—EPHESIANS 5:15–16

The LORD is good,
A stronghold in the day of trouble.

—NAHUM 1:7

And from the days of John the Baptist until now the kingdom of heaven suffers violence [attacks], and the violent take it [overcome their enemies] by force.

—MATTHEW 11:12

Note: We must bring the kingdom of heaven to the earth for the will of God to be done.

Your kingdom come.
Your will be done.

—MATTHEW 6:10

Therefore do not worry about tomorrow, for tomorrow will worry about its own things. Sufficient for the day is its own trouble.

—MATTHEW 6:34

If I take the wings of the morning [the pinnacle or highest point of the morning] . . .

—PSALM 139:9

This is the way of those who are foolish . . .
The upright shall have dominion over them in the morning.

—PSALM 49:13–14

I rise before the dawning of the morning,
And cry for help;
I hope in Your word.
My eyes are awake through the night watches,
That I may meditate on Your word.

—PSALM 119:147–148

Then God said, "Let there be lights . . . and let them be for lights in the firmament of the heavens to give light on the earth"; and it was so. Then God made two great lights: the greater light to rule the day, and the lesser light to rule the night.

—GENESIS 1:14–16

You are all sons of light and sons of the day.

—1 THESSALONIANS 5:5

You are the light of the world.

—MATTHEW 5:14

You have made him [man] to have dominion over the works of Your hands;
You have put all things under his feet [the seat of our authority].

—PSALM 8:6, CF. JOSHUA 1:3

But to you who fear My name
The Sun of Righteousness [Jesus] shall arise
With healing in His wings....
You shall trample the wicked,
For they shall be ashes under the soles of your feet.

—MALACHI 4:2–3

Thus says the LORD,
Who gives the sun for a light by day,
The ordinances of the moon and the stars for a light by
    night...
"If those ordinances depart
From before Me, says the LORD,
Then the seed of Israel shall also cease
From being a nation before Me forever."

—JEREMIAH 31:35–36

Then God said, "Let there be lights in the firmament of the heavens to divide the day from the night; and let them be for signs and seasons, and for days and years.

—GENESIS 1:14

Hear, O our God, for we are despised; turn their reproach on their own heads, and give them as plunder to a land of captivity! [Nehemiah reversed the curse.]

—NEHEMIAH 4:4

For we do not wrestle against flesh and blood, but against principalities [chief devils], against powers [demonic special agents], against the rulers of the darkness of this age [world cosmetic deceivers], against spiritual hosts of wickedness in the heavenly places [spirits of degeneration].

—EPHESIANS 6:12

Note: In Lucifer's fallen state he was still known as a light bringer, daystar, and a son of the morning. These are all counterfeits of the real thing. We are the genuine, and when we become early risers to command the morning and capture the day, we displace the devil.

> How you are fallen from heaven,
> O Lucifer, son of the morning!
> How you are cut down to the ground,
> You who weakened the nations!
>
> —Isaiah 14:12

> If they [God's people] obey and serve Him,
> They shall spend their days in prosperity,
> And their years in pleasures.
>
> —Job 36:11

Note: Every time we rise, we enter into a day that the Lord has made, and we are commanded to rejoice and be glad in it.

> This is the day the Lord has made;
> We will rejoice and be glad in it.
>
> —Psalm 118:24

CHAPTER ELEVEN

The Lines
of the Spirit

*Being Horizontally and Vertically
Lined Up in the Spirit*

IT IS THE summer of 2006 as I am writing this book, and since January of this year God has taken me to new levels in Him. I feel as if I have been restored to my first love with God. If we would be honest enough to admit it, the greatest challenge in Christianity is maintaining our first love. It is so easy to get lacka-daisical in the things of God because there are so few people who are really excited about the deeper things of Him. My heart's desire is to see the greater works that Jesus spoke of firsthand. The Lord is leading me to share with you what has changed my life over the past six months—the revelation of the "lines of the Spirit."

One morning I was awakened by God to prepare for a regular church service. There was nothing special going on. To me it was just another day to praise the Lord. As I began to seek God about the service, He began to show me lines in the Spirit. Some lines were horizontal, and some were vertical.

The Lord told me to use a projector and graph paper to present the vision that God had given me for the congregation. Many people in the service that day had traveled from around the country. I am sure they had urgent needs and were seeking God for deliverance. In the midst of this, I was teaching on a number line. My topic was "Tapping Into the Coordinates of God." God showed me that if believers would follow His coordinates, they would pinpoint the will of God for their lives. I call this understanding, my "place called *There*."

The Greek word for *place* is *topos*, and it refers to a place or position of opportunity. This is another word for *coast*. God promised Joshua that he would achieve victory as long as he stayed in his coast. (See Joshua 1:1–9.) The *topos* is the place that is licensed for promise.

This reminds me of a zoning approval for a business. When you are approved by the zoning commission of the city, you can legally operate as a business. When we get in the place that God has legally set aside for us, everything that we put our hands to the plow to do will prosper! This is when we hit the bull's-eye of the will of God!

Ephesians 4:27 warns us not to give place to the devil. This word *place* is *topos*. I would like to look at this passage from another perspective. If a devil in place can prosper, how much more can a blood-bought, born-again believer (in place) prosper? There are no limits when we line up with the coordinates of God.

God used the coordinates of the number line to give me a revelation of lines of the Spirit. It has changed how I view the spirit realm, and it has affected my life forever. The Lord showed me how people had to be horizontally and vertically lined up to fulfill their destiny in life. I saw lines that came from the third heaven down to earth. There were also lines that were connected across the earth. The Lord said to me that if His people would get in place (line up), doors would be opened for them that no man could deny. With this word, God commanded me to get in place! He said that I would experience the benefits of an open heaven like never before. I call this being spiritually, vertically lined up.

He also warned me that I had to be connected with the right people and disconnected from the wrong people in the earth realm. He showed me that covenant relationship would mean everything in this hour! I knew in my spirit that I could not waste time yoking up with people just to be doing it. I have just turned forty-five years old, and it seems like I was only twenty-five years old yesterday. What's my point? I am not getting younger, and I only have one life to live. I have purposed to spend it seeking the perfect will of God.

Reader, you need to stop and evaluate your relationships now. The greatest warfare you can go through is being connected with people that God has not called you to be with. Being unequally yoked does not just relate to marriage. There are things in my life that were held back until certain people moved on!

I am not promoting cliques with so-called successful people. The purpose of what God was showing me was not about "who's who in the Spirit." It is simply about "whom God is connecting us with" to fulfill His purpose. The Lord was not telling me to connect with millionaires or movie stars. He was saying that I needed to hook up with people who were going somewhere in the Spirit.

In the last days the people of God must have an eye in the Spirit. People who appear to be going places in the natural are not even moving. It only counts if we are gaining ground in the Spirit. God showed me that it was urgent that His people not be distracted by relationships out of time, season, or even the will of God. He told me to evaluate my relationships, because I would only be able to go as far as the people who were around me.

Faith comes by hearing, but the Bible also says that we can only have as much as we can see. (See Genesis 15:5.) If we can only see people who are struggling with never-ending issues and not willing to do something significant in God, we will end up just like them.

CELEBRATE SHAKERS AND MOVERS

I have made up my mind not to be bound by the status quo! It is the status quo of Christianity to wander around in the wilderness of life and never achieve the abundance that God has promised us. Times are hard in the days that we live in, but they are producing a generation of shakers and movers. These are people that God will use to shake everything that can be shaken and to move every mountain that the devil places in their way.

I thank God that He has connected me with people in my life who are shakers and movers. Their ability to shake and move is rooted in the fact that they are vertically and horizontally lined up! I get joy in seeing my brothers and sisters in the Lord achieve great things. This also strengthens me to be an achiever. Greatness gives birth to greatness, and the more we celebrate each other, the greater we become as individuals.

This was the case with Mary and Elizabeth. Both of them were pregnant with greatness on the inside. Mary was pregnant with Jesus, and Elizabeth with John the Baptist. They did not fight the greatness on the inside of each other, but instead they celebrated each other. What was in Mary was strategically connected to what was in Elizabeth to perform the perfect will of God. They were vertically and horizontally lined up with the will of God.

Through angelic visitations from heaven and earthly connection to each other, they knew the perfect will of God! Zacharias, John the Baptist's father, wrestled with the lines of the Spirit when the angel visited him about the birth of his son. He disagreed with destiny, and the angel shut his mouth until he lined up with the will of God. (See Luke 1:11–25.) Many people are out of alignment with the things of the Spirit. They miss God's best for their lives because of doubt, insecurity, and jealousy. They do not know who they are, and as a result, they are afraid to be around people who are superachievers. They are only comfortable in settings where their achievements are highlighted.

Some leaders in the body of Christ fear having people around them that shake and move for Jesus. A wise leader surrounds himself or herself with people who are go-getters! This is the spirit of the Father, who delights in seeing His children do greater than He has done. Even Jesus said that we, as believers, would do greater works than He has done (John 14:12).

I have ministered deliverance to many people who were in bondage to another man's success. They asked God, "When is my time coming?" This is the wrong question to ask God when your brother or sister is being blessed. Instead, we should celebrate each other with clear hearts and minds.

If you get negative feelings when you see someone being blessed, you need to ask God to deliver you now. You know what I am talking about! As soon as your friend tells you about his or her promotion, you have to do everything you can to pretend that you are happy for them because you are not. The reason that you are not happy is because you feel as though your promotion at your job is three years late in coming. What you need to know is that the thing in your heart that will not celebrate your friend's promotion is probably what is holding your promotion back.

If you do not struggle with these negative feelings, there may be people around you who do. Pray for them! It is time for us to check our hearts and our surroundings and line up for the End-Time harvest that is being released. Get in place so that the lines of the Spirit will fall upon you.

THE LINES ARE FALLEN UPON YOU

Psalm 16:5–6 (AMP) declares this:

> The Lord is my chosen and assigned portion, my cup; You hold and maintain my lot. The lines have fallen for me in pleasant places; yes, I have a good heritage.

This is a powerful passage. When I read this scripture, I received a better revelation of the lines of the Spirit. I understood that I have personal lines in the Spirit that work for me. The Hebrew word for *lines* is *chebel.* It refers to our lot or measured inheritance in life. *Chebel* is our portion! Like everything else in God, this is conditional. The psalmist began by saying that the Lord was his portion. We cannot experience the benefits of *chebel* without God being our sole portion.

This knowledge ought to cause you to begin rejoicing right now! Even if nothing ever goes the way that I want it to...JESUS IS MY PORTION! The subtle understanding to this is that things will work out for my good because I love the Lord and am called *according* to His purpose (Rom. 8:28)! The key words are *His purpose.* My portion secures His purpose for my life!

The Greek word for *purpose* is *prothesis,* and it means "the proposal and intentions that God has set forth for our lives." It amazes me how believers seem to think that they know what is better for them than the Creator Himself. Jesus walked the earth realm and always reminded people that He did not come to do His will but the will of the Father. The permissive will of God is a religious cliché in the church. I dare to pursue *the perfect will of God for my life!* This may sound like a strong statement, but it is easier to understand what I mean when you have a revelation of what the perfect will of God really is.

> And do not be conformed to this world, but be transformed by the renewing of your mind, that you may prove what is that good and acceptable and perfect will of God.
> —ROMANS 12:2

It is important to understand what the Bible means by "the good and acceptable and perfect will of God." There are three stages of the will of God:

- The *good will* (*agathos*): This is the beginning stages of the will of God. The word *agathos* means "benefit."

There are benefits in blind obedience to the will of God. At this stage you are really walking by faith and not by sight. This is the stage in the will of God when you do not lean to your own understanding but acknowledge Him in all your ways, and He will direct your path. (See Proverbs 3:5.)

- The *acceptable will* (*euarestos*): This is the stage in the will of God when a person begins to come into agreement with God's will. *Euarestos* means "to be fully agreeable and well pleasing." When Psalm 6:16 speaks of the lines (your lot in life) falling in pleasant places, that Hebrew word is *naweem,* and it means "sweet and agreeable places." When we come in agreement with the acceptable will of God, we get in place to receive our lot in life.

- The *perfect will* (*teleios*): This is the will of God in its completed stage. *Teleios* means "to be complete in labor, growth, and mental and moral character." This is the stage where a person experiences growth and maturity. That person knows with everything within that he or she is in the perfect will of God. He may not know all the details, but he knows that he is in the right place, at the right time, doing the right thing, with the right people. Hallelujah! This knowing brings forth strong mental and moral character.

By now the statement "The lines are fallen for me!" should have a brand-new meaning to you. When the lines of the Spirit fall for you, there is nothing that can prevent your season. You literally step into the set time of God. This is a place where there are no variables that can influence your lot in life. Acts 1:26 reminds us that as they were looking for a twelfth apostle, the lot fell on Matthias. There was no doubt that he was the "chosen one." As we line up with the will of God, nothing that God has for us will be held back. We do not have to cheat, step on other people, or try to push our way to the front of the line. Getting at the front of the lines of men cannot compare to getting under the "lines of the Spirit"! This is called *walking circumspectly*.

> See then that you walk circumspectly, not as fools but as wise, redeeming the time, because the days are evil. Therefore do not be unwise, but understand what the will of the Lord is.
> —EPHESIANS 5:15–17

The word *circumspectly* is *akribos,* and it means "to walk exactly or perfectly." As I mentioned earlier, this means being in the right place, at the right time, doing the right thing, with the right people! There is a perfect will of God, and when we line up with His precision, we can experience it. The perfect will of God can be our portion when we become sensitive to the *time* and *place* of God.

To walk in the perfect will of God, we must sanctify ourselves. Sanctification is not as deep a concept as religion tries to make it. It simply means to separate ourselves unto God. To separate unto God means that we must separate ourselves from some people. To do this, you may even have to hurt somebody's feelings. Do not fret; walk circumspectly! Clear the space that God has given you from unauthorized people. Do not allow squatters to fill the space God has given you in life.

The devil will send others in to distract you and crowd your purpose. Avoid them, and be horizontally lined up with the will of God. Remember, vertical alignment is being under an open heaven, and horizontal alignment is having the right connections in the earth realm. When you line up or walk circumspectly, it redeems your time! When your time is redeemed, everything that has been stolen from you concerning your *kairos* (season) is recovered and fulfilled.

THERE REALLY IS A STAIRWAY TO HEAVEN

As I began to study more on the lines of the Spirit, God reminded me of Jacob's ladder. In Genesis 28:12, Jacob fell into a vision where he saw angels descending and ascending.

I thought, *That's it . . . the lines from heaven were like Jacob's ladder!* When I researched the word *ladder*, I found it is *cullam*; it means "stairway." The Bible says that this ladder was connected to heaven, but it touched down on earth. God promised me that He would give me revelation to bring heaven down to earth. He showed me that this is the only way we can walk in dominion in the earth realm. The kingdom has to come so that God's will can be done on earth as it is in heaven.

I began to pray, "God, mirror heaven to the earth!" This can only happen when we use the authority that Jesus gave us to bind and loose. I saw the angels bringing things to earth that have been loosed or allowed. They were also taking things away that have been bound or forbidden.

As we command our mornings and capture our days, we must have a vision of what is going on in the spirit realm. When we are praying, if we cannot see it, it will never come to us. There really is a stairway to heaven! When we are lined up with it, we can have whatever we say, but we must be able to see it first.

Lately I have had a greater revelation of the statement "It is already done!" I have sung, preached, and prophesied it, but today I have a revelation of it. Judges 5:20 opened my eyes:

> They fought from the heavens;
> The stars from their courses fought against Sisera.

This scripture is referring to Deborah and Barak and their battle against Sisera. Barak asked Deborah to go into battle with him. She agreed, but said that a woman would get the credit for the victory. The above scripture is from the song of Deborah after the battle was over. It depicted what was going on behind the scenes of the battle.

First it says that the battle was not fought from the earth, but from heaven! It literally says that the stars (princes) fought Sisera on behalf of God's people. The Hebrew word for *stars* relates to angelic reinforcements. By the time Sisera got to Jael's tent, the battle was already won. The prince angels had taken him out.

What a revelation of "It's already done!" All Jael had to do was line up and get in place. She was in her place (*topos*), and her victory was already established in the heavens. The angels were lined up in their courses, and Jael was under an open heaven.

The word *courses* in the Hebrew tongue is *mecillah,* and it is a path or stairway that came down from heaven to earth. New faith has risen in my belly since I grabbed hold of this scripture. People in religious settings will fight this kind of teaching, because it is not familiar to them. Religious people are still waiting on the Messiah to show up for the first time, so it does not matter. You have to know the will of God for yourself! People are afraid to deal in the heavens. It is not a popular teaching in the church, so people cannot relate.

Because most Christians agree that we have guardian angels assigned to us, I would like to pose this question: Can the angels be watching over us from the heavens? Are these the lines spoken of in Psalms? Is this why the angels were in their courses over Deborah and Barak? I can verify that this is where Michael fought the prince of Persia on Daniel's behalf (Dan. 10:13). It was fought from the heavens!

I did a word search on the word *stars*, and everywhere I saw it in the Old Testament it referred to an angel. The Hebrew word is *kowkab*, and it means "prince or angel." In Isaiah 14:13, when Lucifer said that he wanted to exalt himself above the stars of God, he was speaking of the prince angels of God.

I pray that this revelation will change the way you pray. Do not be afraid to acknowledge angels in your warfare. They are really the ones fighting the battle behind the scenes. As we bind and loose, things do not just haphazardly happen. Angels are really working on our behalf! The basic principle of binding and loosing is commanding angelic beings on behalf of the will of God in the earth.

There are demonic forces of principalities and powers of the air, but the good news is that there are more *for* us than *against* us. Only one-third of the angels fell from glory with Lucifer. Two-thirds are waiting for our command to fight battles on our behalf. Use the life and death in the dominion of your tongue to release them to their assignments. I believe that every time we speak the Word of God, angels are released to reinforce it. On the other hand, whenever we speak doubt, demons have the right of way to be dispatched. Angels reinforce life, and demons reinforce death.

So, for the past six months, God has been dealing with me about lining up with my destiny. God has put a demand on me to not be comfortable with where I have been. Six months ago my ministry did not own any major properties. We were renting the building that we have been in for eleven years, and we owned a few houses.

Since I have obeyed the Lord in becoming an early riser and commanding my mornings, all of this has changed. Not only has God blessed us with new levels of power, but He has also blessed us with new levels of provision. We have recently been approved for a three-million-dollar building project, and all of our debts up to 2006 will be totally cleared off the records. We now own the building we were renting. When we first moved into the building, a prophet prophesied that the building would be ours, but at the time it was tied up in red tape. As we commanded our mornings and captured our days, the red tape was removed. The church has also acquired three other major properties during this period. I do not think it is by chance. The lines have fallen upon us. I speak this blessing upon you and your family!

As I mentioned earlier, God has not only blessed my heart, but He has also blessed my loins. My children are blessed! I have nine-year-old twins that will be doing major movie projects in Hollywood anytime now. I mentioned that my oldest son is being featured on an HBO special earlier in this book. As we speak, BET (Black Entertainment Television) is also working on a feature story about his testimony. When the lines of the Spirit fall upon you, it will get even the world's attention and souls will be won.

More than anything else I am proud to say that my children are not depressed with life. All of them love Jesus and enjoy having a family on the front lines of ministry. It is important that as God is blessing us, our children are not left out. After the children of Israel were released from Egypt, they wandered around in the wilderness for forty years. During those forty years none of their children were circumcised. Before Joshua could go into the Promised Land, he had to circumcise the generation that grew up in the wilderness. We cannot go into the blessings of the Lord without the lines falling upon our seed. Like anyone else, our family has circumstances and situations that we really have to keep on the altar of God. Despite our challenges, we do not have time to focus on what the devil is doing. God is doing great things! He is doing great things in me AND IN MY SEED! As you line up with Him and open your eyes, this will be easier to see. I pray that my testimonies will bless you, and I command you to rise to the occasion and allow the lines of the Spirit to connect you to your destiny. It will bless you from your present need to your future seed!

CHAPTER TWELVE

The Ordinances of the Lord

God's Order Is Established Forever

Then God said, "Let there be lights in the firmament of the heavens to divide the day from the night; and let them be for signs and for seasons, and for days and years.

—GENESIS 1:14

Thus says the LORD,
Who gives the sun for a light by day,
The ordinances of the moon and the stars for a light by night,
Who disturbs the sea,
And its waves roar
(The LORD of hosts is His name):

"If those ordinances [of fixed order] depart from before Me,
    says the LORD,
Then the seed of Israel shall also cease
From being a nation before Me forever."

—JEREMIAH 31:35–36

THE SCRIPTURES LISTED above declare that there is a fixed order in the heavens that has been established by God. It is clear that the sun and moon were fixed in the heavens for signs and seasons, days and years. Let's review the significance of each:

1. *Signs* (*'owth*)—a sign is that which appears in the sky as evidence of supernatural occurrences. It can be a miracle, signal, beacon, or omen.

2. *Seasons* (*mowed'*)—season is an appointed time.

3. *Days* (*yowm*)—daily chronicles in life.

4. *Years* (*shaneh*)—a year is a revolution in time.

God has set order in the heavens that relates to the occurrences listed above. By His Word, He confirms that there are ordinances fixed in the heavens, and they shall never depart from Him. He says that if they depart from Him, Israel will cease to be a nation before Him. We know that this will never happen because Israel is the apple of God's eye. In Psalm 89:34–35, God swears by His holiness (which cannot be violated) that David's offspring shall endure forever and his throne shall continue before the Lord, just as the sun is before Him. This is a covenant that God made with David. It did two things:

1. Assured Israel's endurance

2. Sealed the fact that the ordinances of the Lord would be established in the heavens forever

Psalm 119:89–91 tell us that the Word of God is settled in the heavens forever and that He is faithful from generation to generation. It also states that the whole universe serves the Lord and continues to do so according to His ordinances.

WHAT ARE THE ORDINANCES OF THE LORD?

In Jeremiah 33:24–26, God spoke of the appointed ordinances in the whole order of nature. In Job 38:33, God asked Job if he knew the ordinances of heaven and whether he could establish them in the earth realm. It was important to God that men understood the ordinances that He had established in heaven. Colossians 2:14 talks about how Jesus blotted out the handwriting of ordinances that were against us when He died on the cross. This particular word, *ordinance,* is *dogma,* and it means "laws or decrees." The enemy had decreed our doom because of Adam's fall. The demonic destiny that was written in the heavens against man was erased on the cross. The *cheirographon* (handwriting that was against us, Col. 2:14) was replaced by the *kethab* (Exod. 31:18) of God! The *kethab* is the prescribed writing or that which has been written by the one who is authorized. God knows the prescription that Creation needed, and He established it in the heavens by His own hand.

God is calling the twenty-first-century church to a level of warfare that brings heaven down to earth. We must pray prayers that will fill the prescription that God has for the earth. Understanding the ordinances of the Lord is the only way that this can happen. Webster defines an *ordinance* as "authoritative rule or law commanded by injunction and ordained by destiny." The key word in dealing with the ordinances of the Lord is *ordain.* The ordinances of God were ordained before the foundation of the world. They are settled in the heavens. When something is ordained, it has been set in order or put in a position.

God established His laws in the heavens before the creation of time. This is why believers have the right to petition the courts of heaven to override decisions that are made on the earth. The court of heaven is the ultimate supreme court. It is the court of appeals for the born-again believer. One of the Hebrew words for *ordinance* is *koke,* and *Strong's Concordance* gives several words that relate to it:

- Statute
- Custom
- Decree
- Due law
- Portion set

Koke also means appointment of time, space, and labor. Based on this information, ordinances are legal rights that have been established in the heavens by God. They relate to appointed times that have been set in the heavens. This is why it is important to live under an open heaven. There are things that have been established in the heavens that people will not experience because they live under a closed heaven.

I am not talking about people who lived for the devil and never accepted Jesus in their lives. I am referring to saints who never walked in the authority that God gave them permission to walk in on earth. They will go to heaven, but they will never experience "heaven on earth." When we get in place for the kingdom to come, the will of God manifests itself on earth.

There are demonic barricades set up in the second heaven to block the will of God on earth. No matter how hard they try, demons cannot stop that which has been given an appointment in the heavens by God concerning the set time of God. This is the unconditional fulfillment of the fullness of time. It is not influenced by variables. The set time of God is not influenced by people, places, or things. In actuality, God is in total control, and people, places, and things will line up with Him. They cannot be under the influence of anything but the perfect timing of God.

The set time is different from a season. The *kairos* timing of God is a type of season. A Hebrew word that relates to *kairos* is *eth,* and it comes from another Hebrew word, *gehth. Eth* is one word with three principles of time:

1. *The regular event*—these are things bound by chronological time. They are predictable and recur.

2. *The un-recurring event*—these are things that only happen in seasons. It is when things happen at the appropriate time because variables may affect them. An example is when I gave birth to twins. There could not be a set time of delivery because certain variables could influence it. I was carrying two babies.

3. *The set time*—this time is not influenced by variables. Circumstances and situations cannot change it. An example of set time is when Jesus was born in Bethlehem. Every detail of His birth was established in the heavens. All circumstances and situations had to line up. The set time was written in the stars, and the wise men picked it up as they were studying the constellations. Mary and Joseph had to move to Bethlehem, and there had to be no room in the inn. It was established in the heavens before time.

It is true! There are ordinances that have been established in the heavens by God that cannot be altered. The only thing that can be altered is our part in them. God gave us the most valuable thing in the earth realm—a will! The will of man is valuable because it has the ability to make us or break us. How we use our will in the earth determines where we will spend eternity. Jesus had to renounce His will so that He could finish what He came to do in the earth. Jesus had to line up with what was ordained for Him on the earth in heaven.

> The heavens declare the glory of God;
> And the firmament shows His handiwork.
> Day unto day utters speech,
> And night unto night reveals knowledge.
> There is no speech nor language
> Where their voice is not heard.
> Their line is gone out through all the earth,

And their words to the end of the world.
In them He has set a tabernacle for the sun.

—PSALM 19:1–4

This scripture tells us that the heavens speak forth the mysteries of God daily and show His knowledge nightly. The Amplified Version of the Bible says that the "voice [in evidence]" of the stars goes "through all the earth...to the end of the world." Many believers would put on the brakes when people speak of the mysteries of God in the constellations because they are quick to relate it to horoscopes. Horoscopes are the devil's perversion of the zodiac that was originally created by God. (See Job 38:32, AMP.) Romans 10:18 speaks of the voice of nature bearing God's message to the ends of the world.

GOD'S ZODIAC

Can you bind the chains of [the cluster of stars called] Pleiades, or loose the cords of [the constellation] Orion? Can you lead forth the signs of the zodiac in their season? Or can you guide [the stars of] the Bear with her young? Do you know the ordinances of the heavens? Can you establish their rule upon the earth?

—JOB 38:31–33, AMP

When I first discovered this passage it blew my mind. I thought, *God created the zodiac!* I hate the devil. He twists and turns everything to confuse the people of God so that they can never tap in to what God has for them in life on earth. In the King James Version of this passage the word for *zodiac* is *Mazzaroth*. Through this chapter, God is naming some of the constellations of the heavens. A constellation is a group of named stars that are fixed in the heavens.

Again, I want to emphasize that I realize the context of Job 38 is God's correction of Job. However, I would like to take note that all of the things that God named in this chapter indicated what *He* had done. Therefore, we need to know that God has a purpose for the constellations in relation to the earth. God did not initiate the horoscope, but He created the zodiac. His mysteries are written in the stars. Evil people have perverted His plan for the constellations for their own wicked purposes. Horoscopes are charts that astrologers read based on the position of the planets in order to tell a person his or her future. It is an abomination, because men attempt to overlook God and depend on the stars instead of on Him.

These people actually worship the constellations, because they know that there is information in the stars. It is important to note the difference in the words *astrology* and *astronomy*. Astrology is soothsaying, and astronomy is the science of studying the stars. Many people in the profession of astronomy cross over into the realm of astrology because of ignorance.

THE MINISTRY OF THE STARS

I mentioned earlier that every Old Testament word for *stars* has been defined as *princes*. This means that the stars spoken of are representative of prince angels. Even in Revelation 12:4 it speaks of how the tail of the dragon swept across the sky and drew down one-third of the stars. This scripture also references angels. Revelation 1:20 speaks of the mystery of the seven stars. It reveals that the seven stars are the seven angels of the seven churches. Angels are so significant in the lives of people that there was an angel assigned over each of the seven churches that John addresses in Revelation.

Take a look at the statement that Lucifer made in Isaiah 14:13: "I will ascend into heaven, I will exalt my throne above the stars of God." This word *stars* also means "princes," and is *kowkab* in Hebrew. Lucifer wanted to exalt himself above all the angels of God and ultimately be higher than God Himself.

The Bible teaches that God created the sun to rule over the day, and the moon and stars to rule by night (Ps. 136:8–9). The Hebrew word for *rule* is *memshalah,* which means "to have supreme authority." The word *stars* in this passage means "prince angels." Based on this, it is safe to say that the angels that have charge over us are ruling spirits in the heavens.

Psalm 91:11 says that God gives His angels charge over us to keep us in all our ways. This word *charge* is *tsavah,* and it means "to appoint a messenger." Psalm 19:4 speaks of the lines of angels that go throughout the earth to the end of the world. The meaning of the word *lines* is a cord that measures. It means to have rule or influence over. We often overlook the ministry of angels. I am sure most people do not relate them to the stars. There are courses or lines in the Spirit whereby angels have dominion to rule. This is their ministry. I believe that when we bind and loose in spiritual warfare, we release angels to move on our behalf or against our foes.

There are many kinds of angels:

- *Ministering angels.* These are the angels that ministered to Jesus after His experience in the wilderness.

- *Warring angels.* This is the angelic reinforcement that Daniel received against the prince of Persia and Greece.

- *Worshiping angels.* The Bible speaks of angelic beings that worship God continuously.

- *Guardian angels.* Psalm 91:1 tells us of the angels that have charge over us.

- *Messenger angels.* Gabriel was the angel that God used to send a message about the birth of Jesus.

- *Destiny angels.* God told the children of Israel that He would send an angel before them. This angel could not be provoked on the way. I call this the destiny angel.

Apply what you have learned about the ordinances of the Lord and the ministry of angels by praying this prayer with me:

Father God, I believe in the ministry of angels. I thank You for the angels that You have assigned to watch over me and my family. Make me sensitive to their presence. Chain-linked angels are strategically stationed around everything that concerns me. Ministering angels, guardian angels, worshiping angels, messenger angels, and destiny angels, I acknowledge that you exist, and I get in place to receive your ministry.

I renounce the worship of angels or any idolatry that would enter my heart concerning their ministry. I command every demonic ruler that the enemy has assigned to my life to go and be displaced by ruling princes of the Lord. Make my ears sensitive to the words that creation is speaking concerning the will of God in the earth realm.

I command the kingdom to come and the will of God to be done on earth as it is in heaven. Let everything in my life be removed that will get me off course. I abide under the course of the princes of God, and no second heaven activity has rule over me. All demonic cords are cut, and the rule of the Most High God is established over my head. I am living under an open heaven. The angels are descending and ascending on my behalf. I am apostolically lined up to fulfill my part in the ordinances of God designed in heaven.

CHAPTER THIRTEEN

Spiritual Authority
in the Army
of the Lord (Part 1)
Preparing to Be Combat Ready

As you may have noticed, this book has a strong military flavor. The Lord blessed me to spend six years and eight months in the United States Army. Though I thought I had gone to hell when I arrived at basic training, it was the best thing that ever happened to me. I describe my experience in my book *Delivered to Destiny*.

The things that I learned in the army will forever be a part of me. I was taught discipline, order, and consistency. These things were not a part of my upbringing, and it really helped me to get a grip on life. When I got saved, a light bulb came on in my head. I believe that God put me in the natural military to make me a better soldier for the Lord. I was always a fighter, but the military put some structure and order to my ability to fight.

In the kingdom of God, many of the same principles that Uncle Sam taught me still apply. After I swore in at the army processing center, the army had the responsibility of turning a crackhead into a valiant soldier. As I look back, it reminds me of Gideon. God called him "a mighty man of valor," but he did not know who he was (Judg. 6:12). His focus was on his background, and he could not see how God was about to use him.

I felt the same way! I saw sharp soldiers, and I could not see myself ever walking in their shoes. Their faces showed extreme authority, and they seemed to know who they were in the army. I pray that through reading this chapter, you will get a better revelation of who you are in God. It is all about authority. Power is perfected by authority. Many cannot display the power that has been given to them in God because they do not understand their spiritual authority.

The United States has the greatest military force in the world. When you join the army, its leaders teach you who you are as a soldier. They give you rank as you grow, and with these promotions come new levels of authority. As believers, we are a part of a force much greater than the natural army. The armed forces of the Lord were instituted by God's rule. We bring forth the things of the kingdom of God! The smallest baby in the Lord's army has authority over all the power of the enemy. Turn your spiritual receiver on, and get in the position of attention! Have an ear to hear what the Lord is saying to you concerning your spiritual authority.

THE POSITION OF ATTENTION

Soldiers stand in the position of attention when they receive commands. Each soldier must have an ear to hear what the person giving the command is saying. Oh, how important it is to have an ear to hear in the army of the Lord. Revelation 2:17 says, "He who has an ear, let him hear what the Spirit says to the churches."

In the military, when the leader of the formation calls the group to attention, all commotion must stop. He gives a *preparatory command* that addresses the group so that they will know to whom he is speaking. He calls them by name. His command may be "group," "company," "battalion," or whatever title is appropriate for those he is addressing at the time. This tells the soldiers to cease all activity in the formation and to prepare to hear the command.

Many cannot receive instruction from God because they do not prepare to hear His command. We must be ready when He calls our name. Too often we have set aside time with God and have not given Him the opportunity to speak to us. We spend all of our prayer time talking and never setting time aside to hear Him. This puts God in a box in our lives.

Many do not understand that because we have a will, we can box God off in our lives. Being *combat ready* is being in a place to hear God at any time.

The first thing that an army unit sets up upon deployment is communication. Without communication to headquarters, a unit cannot function. God wants the lines of communication to be open to Him 24/7. No matter when He calls our name, we need to stop what we are doing and get in the position of attention. God is not limited to our prayer times, and because He is the Commander in Chief, He has the right to interrupt us anytime in our day!

Once the leader of a formation gets the attention of the group, a *command of execution* is released. This prompts the soldiers to execute the command given immediately. For example, the preparatory command may be "Company," and the command of execution may be "Attention." At the command of attention, the soldier must be standing still with both hands locked at his side. His eyes must be fixed directly on the leader of the formation in front of him. The soldier is now ready to receive orders. Spiritually speaking, we must be prepared to get in the position of attention, put our eyes on Jesus, and hear what the Spirit of the Lord is saying to the church. Church . . . attention!

THE TIMING OF GOD

I am amazed at how many things from the natural army can be related to God's army. God's army is an army of discipline. Without discipline, there is no true authority. True authority originated between God and man in the garden. When Adam lost his authority through disobedience, Jesus gave it back through obedience. We need more discipline in the church. It prompts obedience.

Most of the time we want to obey God, but the enemy called *procrastination* robs us of the opportunity. Discipline destroys the procrastination that gives power to the flesh to disobey God. If we do not move out in the timing of God, what we do does not count.

There are a few military commands that relate to timing that will illustrate this point:

1. Mark time

To mark time is to march in place and make no progress for a period of time. How many times did God tell His people to stand still? In marking time the soldier is picking his feet up and putting them down but standing in one place. The mistake that many believers make is to do nothing when waiting on God. To spiritually mark time (or stand still) is to wait on God but to move on in life. Even in waiting on God we cannot be idle. To mark time is to march in place until the next command comes. In the meantime, you must do what you can where you are.

A key factor in marking time is that you must stay in cadence with the other soldiers, because you are in a formation. You are not on your own. One can put a thousand to flight; two, ten thousand (Deut. 32:30). Whenever you can touch and agree with another, great things will happen. The word *touch* in Matthew 18:19 literally means "to form a circuit." Circuits ensure a steady flow. While we are waiting on God, we can be assured He is moving behind the scenes. As long as we are obedient where we are, we will be prepared to move out when the command is given.

2. Double time

To move out in double time means to pick up the pace. It is not just important to move when God says to move, but we must also move at His momentum. God warned me in January 2006 that it was not the time to move in the momentum of men. Often men will attempt to set God's pace for our lives. We must move with the momentum or moment of force. We cannot move out in the things of God when we feel like it. There is a moment of force, and we have to "ride or die" when it comes.

The word *hustle* is often used only as a negative word. I believe in *godly hustle*, or "hurry up and get it"! I'm not talking about drugs; I'm talking about the will of God! This kind of hustle is nothing but a spiritual double time in which you are required to pick up the pace. This means you have to deal with particular issues at a faster pace, because you have a quickening order from the Holy Ghost.

God once gave me a revelation about an investment through a supernatural source. I procrastinated, and as a result, when I finally made the investment, I paid almost double the amount per share. The investment was still profitable, but nothing in comparison to what it could have been if I had moved out in the timing of God. Many people have to settle for God's second best because they did not flow with the moment of force. I have adapted a little slang to apply here: If you are slow, you blow it; if you cruise, you lose; you have to mildew or barbecue to get God's best for you!

3. Quick time

When the leader of the formation gives a command of "quick time," this means to run. There is a time to run with the vision. Habakkuk 2:2 says to write the vision down and run with it! This means to make it plain. You can run with a vision that is plain to you. But unless you know where you are going, it is hard to move at this pace. People who have captured the vision can run with it. In the end it shall not lie!

Then the LORD answered me and said:

"Write the vision
And make it plain on tablets,
That he may run who reads it.
For the vision is yet for an appointed time;
But at the end it will speak, and it will not lie,
Though it tarries, wait for it;
Because it will surely come,
It will not tarry."

—HABAKKUK 2:2–3

The word *run* in this scripture is *ruwts* in the Hebrew, which means "to rush." Can I use my own terminology? . . . bum-rush! *Ruwts* actually means "to break and run speedily for whatever reason." *Strong's Exhaustive Concordance* also says that it means "to become a footman that has broken loose and stretched out." When God gives you a quick-time command, He literally transforms your feet and gives you the ability to run. Second Samuel 22:34, Psalm 18:33, and Habakkuk 3:19 all say that God gives us hinds' feet and sets us upon high places. In the Hebrew language, the words that relate to the word *hinds* are:

- *Ayal—* to run like a stag or male ram
- *Ayalah*—to run like a female doe

I can only interpret this one way. Whether you are male or female, you can run with the vision of God. Notice that the scripture denotes that the vision is only for an appointed time. When the "appointed time" comes . . . run! The man who cannot run with the vision when the command is given will be left behind.

ACCOUNTABILITY OR CONFINEMENT?

When I was stationed in Frankfurt, Germany, we usually had three formations a day. One was for physical training at 5:00 a.m.; the next was to report to work at 8:00 a.m. The last formation of the day was to end the workday. All of these formations instilled accountability. Uncle Sam wanted to know where his soldiers were at all times.

We were often reminded that our lives were not our own. God keeps up with His soldiers better than Uncle Sam. As soon as Adam fell, God came down and asked him, "Where are you?" In military duty, accountability is twenty-four hours a day, seven days a week. This was always instilled in the back of our minds. Though we had work hours and time off, we had to understand that we were always on call.

Isn't it baffling how we think we have done God a favor by giving Him a little time out of our day? God does not want time out of our days; He wants to possess our days totally. In the military, if someone in our chain of command tried to call us in for duty and was unsuccessful, we would be considered AWOL. To be AWOL, or absent without leave, is a serious charge in the military. All enlisted soldiers are governed under what is called the Uniform Code of Military Justice. These are the regulations that govern over the military court system.

Adam was AWOL when God came looking for him in the garden. Adam had broken God's law and was out of place in the spirit. When we willfully continue to break the laws of God, we become spiritual criminals. I grew up criminally minded! I thank God that I laid my criminal mentality down when I came into Christ.

I believe that criminally minded persons are not just rapists, mass murderers, or bank robbers. A criminally minded person is any person not accountable to governing authorities and the laws that have been established under their rule. People who knowingly drive without a driver's license or write bad checks are criminally minded. Law-abiding citizens follow the rules, because they are accountable to them.

Rules do not matter to people who are not accountable. I minister to people from the streets all the time. Most have the same story: they live according to what they can get away with. They drive without licenses, steal gas from filling stations, and have no insurance for their cars! They never sit down and grasp the fact that one day they will be caught.

The most important factor of authority is accountability. God cannot delegate authority to those who are not willing to be accountable. To be accountable is to be obliged to answer for actions or responsible for a fault if it occurs. The prisons are filled with people who were never accountable to anyone. They were rebellious little children who did not obey their parents, and they grew up to be rebellious citizens who would not obey the laws of the land. In prison, inmates have no choice but to obey the "rules of confinement," or the confinement level increases.

The highest level of confinement is to be left alone. Prisons have "holes" or places of solitary confinement for inmates who cannot obey rules. It is the same way in the things of the spirit. There is a spiritual solitary confinement for those who continue to break God's rules even in the midst of His chastisement. This is why people who are being disciplined by God cannot enjoy anything around them until they get it right. Even in the midst of everything they imagined to be great, they are confronted with a solitude that seems unbearable.

The ultimate solitary confinement in life is for those who continue to resist the correction of God and cross the line. This is a line in the spirit that no man wants to cross. It is called *reprobation*! To be reprobate means to be eternally condemned. The Greek word for *reprobate* is *adokimos,* and it means to have a stamp of disapproval from God on one's head. It means to be a marked man. It means to be a castaway who is worthless to God because of eternal rejection from Him.

Is there a biblical example of reprobation? Yes! Cain was the first child born of a woman, the first murderer, and the first man given unto a reprobate mind!

> And [the Lord] said, What have you done? The voice of your brother's blood is crying out to Me from the ground. And now you are cursed by reason of the earth, which has opened its mouth to receive your brother's [shed] blood from your hand. When you till the ground, it shall no longer yield to you its strength; you shall be a fugitive and a vagabond on the earth [in

perpetual exile, a degraded outcast]. Then Cain said to the Lord, My punishment is greater than I can bear. Behold, You have driven me out this day from the face of the land, and from Your face I will be hidden; and I will be a fugitive and a vagabond and a wanderer on the earth, and whoever finds me will kill me. And the Lord said to him, Therefore, if anyone kills Cain, vengeance shall be taken on him sevenfold. And the Lord set a mark or sign upon Cain, lest anyone finding him should kill him. So Cain went away from the presence of the Lord and dwelt in the land of Nod [wandering], east of Eden.

—GENESIS 4:10–16, AMP

Whew! Why don't we have more teaching on this? This scripture speaks of people living on earth who cannot be saved because they are eternally damned. God put a mark on Cain's head, and the word *mark* means "omen." An *omen* is defined as "a curse or a sign of bad luck." Personally I do not believe in bad luck. I believe in blessings and curses! The mark that God put on Cain's head warned men not to touch him, because he had been cursed by God. Talk about solitary confinement! Cain was so confined that his enemies could not even get to him. Vengeance against him was the Lord's!

In Romans 1:28, God turned people over to reprobation because of homosexuality. Today we have preachers who have churches for homosexuals to gather openly and comfortably. These people abide in the land of Nod! *Nod* in the Hebrew is a place of exile or wandering. It is a place for defectors who have left their natural place to join another. Preachers who are ministering the inclusion of those who do things that God has excluded are spiritual defectors. They are wanderers in the earth realm until they meet their ultimate solitary confinement—a lonely burning hell! They are men on spiritual death row.

People with reprobate minds did not start out as heathens. These are people who hang around churches. Second Timothy 3:8 relates people of apostasy (who have fallen away from God) to the warlocks that Moses threw his rod before to swallow their serpents. The scripture says that they are just like witches with reprobate minds that resist the truth. Titus 1:16 (AMP) also confirms that reprobate minds are ignited from playing with God. This state does not come from playing with Ouija boards! It reads:

> They profess to know God [to recognize, perceive, and be acquainted with Him], but deny and disown and renounce Him by what they do; they are detestable and loathsome, unbelieving and disobedient and disloyal and rebellious, and [they are] unfit and worthless for good work (deed or enterprise) of any kind.

The rules of confinement give men no options! Many believers are bound by these spiritual rules of confinement, which bind them because they would not submit their wills to accountability. This is the greatest warfare in spiritual warfare—making the right choices. A foundational choice for every person covered under the blood of Jesus is this:

> Submit your will to accountability, or be incarcerated by the rules of confinement!

This may sound harsh, but it is biblical. Many people are in spiritual prisons because they chose their own way. They did not submit to lawful authority. In the army this is called "failure to obey a lawful command." In the kingdom it is called *blasphemy*! Blasphemy is any word or action that is disrespectful to God or the things that pertain to Him. Paul turned Hymenaeus and Alexander over to the devil's prison so that they would learn not to blaspheme or be disrespectful. (See 1 Timothy 1:20.) Their error in doctrine led them to disrespect the position that Paul walked in. He was an apostle of Jesus Christ—a sent one! To disrespect God's delegated authority is to disrespect God.

CHAPTER FOURTEEN

Spiritual Authority in the Army of the Lord (Part 2)

Be Sure You Have a Covering

S PIRITUAL AUTHORITY IS so important in warfare prayer that I could not say everything that I needed to say about it in one chapter. I thank God for the powerful men and women of God He has brought unto my life. Apostle John Eckhardt, Dr. C. Peter Wagner, Dr. Kingsley Fletcher, Pastor Rod Parsley, Bishop Wallace Sibley, and Bishop Quan Miller have all been spiritual coverings at one time or another for my husband and me.

One of the strongest principles instilled in me as a soldier was to never go outside without a covering over my head. It was unheard of for a soldier in uniform to be caught outside without headgear. The theory was that we were being trained for wartime situations. When I was in the army we wore camouflage headgear. If we were in an area that was green, we wore green camouflage caps. If we were in the desert, we wore vanilla and brown colored caps. The idea was to fit into the scenery just in case the enemy launched an air raid.

The prince of the power of the air rules over the children of disobedience. Believers who have no spiritual covering stick out like a sore thumb to him. Real spiritual authority must be submitted to spiritual authority. In the chain of command, each person should have someone to answer to, no matter how high a rank he or she holds.

In the army we were taught to cover each other. This kind of covering was needed when we maneuvered toward a target. We used the buddy system and moved forth in pairs. Many people attempt to move out in the things of God alone. I will say it again, do not fall prey to becoming a lone ranger or solo soldier! At my church, we use at least two people on prayer assignments. It takes at least two to touch and agree. It is always good to have a dedicated prayer partner to cover you in the spirit when you are moving out in something requiring your back to be covered. Your pastor covers your head, but in spiritual combat, you need peers who will cover your back in ground-level warfare.

It is a scary thing to be in the trenches of life without a trench buddy. I need associates in ministry who do not mind rolling up their sleeves and getting "down and dirty" in the trenches with me. I do not hang out with people who are afraid to get dirty in ministry.

When we trained on tactical maneuvers, one soldier would move forward while the other covered. The assignment of the covering soldier was to shoot at the enemy while his buddy low-crawled under fire. Low-crawling gave the soldier the ability to stay below the bullets. If he lifted his head up under fire, the bullets would surely take him out. This is a very important spiritual principle. Humility will always protect you from the fiery darts of the enemy. If you lift your head up in pride in spiritual warfare, you will become a casualty. God resists the proud and is against them.

It is true that if God is for you, no one can stand against you. On the other hand, if God is against you, who can be for you? You can be sure that if God gives you an assignment, you will be under fire! You need someone to intercede for you. Powerful intercession on the behalf of a brother or sister literally releases bombardments against the enemy, which slows him down. This will allow a brother or sister time to break through. When we stand in the gap for each other, it releases another level of authority. Demons fear prayers that are not selfish and self-motivated. Prayer on the behalf of a peer, which is released with right motives and intentions, confuses darkness.

There is authority in numbers, and when we agree, it increases the authority that already exists. The Bible says that one can take authority over a thousand, and two can take authority over ten thousand (Deut. 32:30). The definition of *authority* is "to have the right to command, determine, and enforce laws that have been set in place by a higher governing entity." Jesus established our authority over our enemies when He died on the cross. He went to hell and took all authority from the devil. He stripped the devil of the keys to death, hell, and the grave. This is the greatest victory ever recorded! Now as believers we can walk in daily victory over every challenge in life.

THREE LEVELS OF AUTHORITY

I have a very good friend, Pastor Maldonado, who pastors a church in Miami, Florida. He is a powerful man of God and has one of the largest Spanish churches in America. He walks in uncommon spiritual authority. He told me something about authority that I will never forget. He said that there are three levels of authority:

1. The authority of obedience
2. Earned authority
3. Resurrection authority

He said that obedience opens the door to authority. This is authority that God gives to those who are faithful in the little things.

As we are faithful in the little things that He gives us to do, we get victories under our belt. This leads to the second level of authority— earned authority. This is the authority that Joshua walked in. Because of the battles that he had won, there was a respect that was given to him as a conqueror.

The Bible says that we are more than conquerors (Rom. 8:37). Many believers will never walk in the anointing of conquering until they get victories under their belt. I cannot imagine having no victory. At least I thought I was having victory in the world, even if I was not. It is a miserable thing to come into Christ and walk in defeat.

Defeat and heaviness are twins in the spirit. A defeated person is open to everything that comes with the spirit of heaviness. Suicide, depression, anxiety, and rejection abide over a person with no victory in his or her life. But the opposite is also true; every time we get new victory, it reinforces more victory. The word goes out in the spirit, and our enemies hear about it. This is why the heathen feared the people of God in biblical times.

The enemies of God know whom God is with and whom He is not with. They fear being in the presence of those whom God is with. This is what I call *the Emmanuel anointing*: "God with us!" If God be with us, who can be against us? This is what is written on the forehead of a victorious child of the King.

The first two levels of authority are rooted in obedience and victory. The devil is defeated by the blood of the Lamb and the word of our testimony. People without testimonies are feeble fools to the dark side. If you cannot tell of the goodness of what God has done for you, your words hold no weight in the spirit.

Victorious believers can stand before hell and declare, "I am an overcomer because I have been through a mess and came out smelling like roses!" This is the earned authority of the Joshua generation. They have earned the right to tell it, and they are not ashamed about it. Every time they tell their testimony, they get stronger in the Spirit. Believers who keep skeletons in their closets have little or no authority. They have a dark cloud of lies hovering over their heads every time they try to step out in God. They cannot go forth because the enemy reminds them of their ugly secret. Ugly secrets suck the authority out of a believer. The spirit of condemnation becomes their covering, and they have no real liberty. I realize that there is a time not to tell things, but on the other hand, there is a time to "tell it"!

RESURRECTION AUTHORITY

The third level of authority that my friend mentioned to me was resurrection authority. He did not expound on it, so I asked the Holy Spirit to give me a revelation of resurrection authority.

God told me that the year 2006 was a year of resurrection. I began to rejoice about things being raised from the dead. I never considered that to resurrect a thing, it had to die first. This revelation soon came as we moved into the year. During the time that I have been a pastor at the church on the corner of Steele and Blue, no member of the congregation had died—in eleven years! We have only buried a few relatives of our members.

Earlier this year, my armor bearer dropped dead. He was forty years old and appeared to be perfectly healthy. He fell dead in his home one evening while I was working in my office. I do not wish to discuss the details of his death. When I received the call that he was dead, I did not believe it. I kept working! They called me back and said, "Apostle, Jessie is dead!"

I told them that he was not dead, and I called the prayer warriors to meet me at the hospital. We were going to pray for him and bring him home. In the past, every time we went to a hospital with a situation, we had left in victory.

When I arrived at the hospital, they gave me a badge that said "Quiet Room." I did not know that this was a room for families who had experienced death. Jessie was lying in a bed with his mouth wide open. His body was still warm, and he had a tube down his throat that was sticking out of his mouth. None of us were crying. We expected Jessie to get up and go home with us that night. I laid hands, quoted scriptures, and commanded his spirit to get back into his body. We prayed for hours.

Finally the hospital authorities told us they had to take the body to the morgue. It seemed as if they hated to tell us that we had to leave the hospital room. We were so persistent about raising him from the dead that we followed the body to the morgue and sat outside trying to figure out how to get inside to continue our prayer efforts. We did everything that we could to stop them from embalming the body. I even made my husband go back to the morgue the next morning to pull Jessie's body from the refrigerated holding place to pray for him again.

My husband came home and said, "Baby, he is dead. We have to prepare for a funeral!" Maybe people thought that we were a bunch of religious kooks, but I could only see Jessie alive. I refused to receive death. The next day, members of the church continued to call, asking if our brother had gotten up yet. I eventually had to tell them, "He did not wake up!"

Regularly I preach about casting out devils, healing the sick, and raising the dead. I have never had death come so close. I lay out before the Lord the entire next day. God spoke to me so clearly! He said that signs, wonders, and miracles would follow His people who would believe Him, but a wicked generation sought after signs.

God began to reveal His dominion to me on another level. He said that if He never worked a miracle in my life again, He was still Lord! He showed me how some people only knew how to declare His lordship when they saw Him move for them. They wickedly sought His signs and never wanted anything to do with Him. He warned me never to question His power when I did not see it manifest. *He said that He was Lord all by Himself!*

I learned a great lesson of victory out of what I considered great defeat. My elders and I were so used to seeing daily victory that God was teaching us that even under the worst of circumstances we must declare *His lordship.*

The week before this incident I had seen blind eyes opened and deaf ears unplugged. For months we had seen people walking out of wheelchairs and babies healed of incurable diseases. Oh, how we celebrated! When Jessie died, I could hear the Lord say, "Will you praise Me now?" Then He took me to His Word concerning the matter:

> Because all those men who have seen My glory and My [miraculous] signs which I performed in Egypt and in the wilderness, yet have tested and proved Me these ten times and have not heeded my voice.
>
> —NUMBERS 14:22, AMP

God then began to show me that there was more to resurrection power than seeing His miracles. Many saw miracles and did not heed His voice. For the anointing of true resurrection authority, we must know Him in the power of His resurrection and in the fellowship of His suffering (Phil. 3:10).

When things do not go as they desire, many so-called powerful people question God. True resurrection authority never questions God. I have made many mistakes in my walk with God, but there is one thing I am not guilty of—asking God *why*. There is a saying that when things get tough, the tough get going. I stand on the truth that the kingdom of God suffers violence, and the violent take it by force.

Three weeks after my armor bearer died, my father died. A few weeks after that, two of my close friends lost their fathers in the same week. My husband and I were going separate ways to funerals. It was as if death swept through our lives. I had never before comprehended that to raise something from the dead, something first has to die!

I wonder if people really understand what they are asking for when they ask God for resurrection authority. Martha met Jesus after Lazarus had died, and she acted as though Jesus came too late. Jesus told her, "Your brother will rise again."

She responded by sounding as though she already knew what Jesus was talking about. She said that she knew that he would be raised in the resurrection.

Jesus said with absolute authority, "I am the resurrection!" He said that whoever believed in Him would live again if they were dead. And whoever believed in Him and was alive would never die. (See John 11.)

Resurrection authority gives us the ability to raise the dead. But deeper than that, we have the Resurrection living on the inside of us. So every time a seed goes into the ground and dies in Christ, because of the Resurrection Himself, that seed gives birth to new life!

I preached at my daddy's funeral and at Jessie's. So many souls were saved, and family members were restored to each other. A relationship with a little sister with whom I had not communicated for years was restored because of my daddy's death. In my autobiography, *Delivered to Destiny,* I talked about the people from Uptown. Many of the people from Uptown were at my daddy's funeral. I gave away books at the funeral and signed them. They all knew that my daddy was proud of me. And, by the way, my daddy gave his life to the Lord on his deathbed after seventy-eight years—now that's resurrection power!

DOMINION WARFARE

My heart's desire is to see the dominion that God gave Adam in the garden restored to the church in the last days. *Dominion* is defined as "the exercise of control in one's territory or sphere of influence." Genesis 1:26 describes man's sphere of influence concerning the dominion that God gave him. I call it *territorial dominion*!

> Let them have dominion over the fish of the sea, over the birds
> of the air, and over the cattle, over all the earth and over every
> creeping thing that creeps on the earth.

Most people do not realize that the power of the enemy operates on the earth, under the earth, under the water, and in the air. This is why God gave us territorial dominion from the beginning. We have dominion over things under the water, in the air, and on and under the earth. In Exodus 20:4 God warns His people not to make any images of things in the heavens above, in the earth beneath, or in the water under the earth. There are spirits that rule on the earth, under the earth, and in the air. God has given us power over all of them. Let's take a look at how they operate.

1. The power of the air

Ephesians 2:2 describes the assignment of the prince of the power of the air. One name for the Greek god of the second heaven is *Zeus*. The second heaven is a demonic headquarters that is strategically set up to control people like puppets on a string. In the spirit, that is exactly how it looks—like a puppet show! Every human being is connected to either the second or third heaven. People who are bound by second heaven activity are connected to the second heaven by demonic strings.

The hydra is the god of recurring curses and is also seated in the heavens. It is one of the constellations or groups of stars that abide in the heavens. The power of the air (or unconscious cycle) is a subliminal bondage, which is controlled from the air. This spirit hides behind the cover of natural habits, and its victims never suspect that they are under its control. Before people are delivered from addictions and habits, demonic strings must be cut in the spirit to sever their alliances with the second heaven. After this, ground-level deliverance can take place.

2. Creeping things on the earth

Ground-level warfare is frontline confrontation with the enemy in the earth realm. To fight an enemy effectively, you must be able to identify him. I find it interesting that the word *creeping* (*remes*) in Genesis 1:28 means "reptile." Satan manifested himself to Eve in the garden, and war was waged on earth. Since the beginning, man has battled the reptilian spirit in the earth. These are demons that manifest themselves in earth. The devil has always manifested himself as a reptile. In Genesis, he manifested himself as a serpent. In Revelation he was depicted as a dragon. Despite the devil's evil efforts, from Genesis to Revelation, God has given us dominion over all the power of the enemy. God has revealed these territorial assignments to us so that we can deal with them in prayer. These are the forces of hell that have been set in the earth to oppose the kingdom of God. They are already defeated foes.

3. Marine spirits

Probably the most controversial topic in spiritual warfare is the topic of water spirits. If God said that there were things to be concerned about under the water, it is so! Neptune is the Roman god of the sea and has been worshiped since the beginning of time. In other cultures, he has many other names. Regardless of the name used, he is the god of the water spirits.

The hydra (see chapter sixteen for an expanded teaching about the hydra) is known as a sea monster in Greek mythology. It is also a type of water spirit. In voodoo cults, a water spirit called the *Loa* is conjured as a sea god. The entire system of the warfare of the sea comes under a territorial spirit called *the queen of the coast.*

The highest level of warfare in the dark realm is led by demons that manifest themselves as females. This is because of ancient spirits of antiquity that worship the womb because of its reproductive ability. These female spirits include the queen of the coast, the queen of heaven, and the queen of hell. They rule in the realms indicated by their names.[1]

4. The gates of hell

The Bible reminds us that the gates of hell shall not prevail against the church (Matt. 16:18). This word *gates* is *pule,* and it means "entrances to hell."

Pluto is the Roman god of the underworld. There are many other names for this god also. The entrances (gates) of hell are vortexes through which demons travel back and forth from earth to the underworld. It is no secret that hell is in the core of the earth. The entrances of hell have been said to flow in a spiraling motion. Many testimonies of those who have had near death experiences tell of a spiral entrance to hell. The word *vortex* in the *American Heritage Dictionary* is defined as "passages that flow in a spiral design."

I believe that the Lord has shown me that the fault lines in the earth are directly related to the vortexes of hell. This is how we do warfare against the natural disaster of earthquakes. We bind the traffic of the demonic gateways that would cause earthquakes.

CHAPTER FIFTEEN

The Forces
of the Lord

Have You Enlisted in God's Armed Forces?

A S I MENTIONED in the last chapter, the forces of darkness are territorially and strategically set up in the air, on the earth, in the water, and under the water. The most powerful principle in spiritual warfare is this: *everything that God has, the devil always counterfeits.*

Lucifer wanted to be worshiped, and a war broke out in heaven. Always remember that the battle is over worship. If you can discern the reason for the battle, you will be able to identify the battle plan of your enemies. Many people do not understand why they are experiencing warfare. Yet everyone has the same root reason for experiencing attack. It is simply because we are made in the image of God. (Ain't nobody mad but the devil.) When the devil was cast out of heaven, he hit the ground mad. Since that time he has strategically set up forces to come against the order of God. Since God has set the order of Creation, the devil counters it with a counterfeit order.

Understanding this principle helps us to counter the plans and strategies that oppose the will of God in the earth realm. Before I go into detail concerning the forces of the Lord, I must first discuss *realms*. The word *realm* is another word for kingdom. A kingdom is any area where one thing is dominant. In the plant kingdom, plants are the dominating force. The same is true with the animal and mineral kingdoms.

Since Creation, God has been methodical and meticulous. He is a God of order. He arranged everything that He created with a clear plan. Before time, the details of how God wanted everything He created to be set in order were already in His mind. God did not just throw the stars in the sky, allowing them to fall wherever they landed. Every star has a designated slot in the sky, and every tree has a specific hole in the ground.

The second commandment of the Ten Commandments identified the realms with which we deal in spiritual warfare. (See Exodus 20:4.) The realm in which we live is, of course, on the earth. This scripture also reveals what is not so obvious to us—the realms that men penetrate to worship foreign gods. Wherever there is worship, *there will also be warfare.*

Based on these observations, I believe that there are four realms on which we need to focus for territorial warfare purposes. They are:

1. The heavens
2. The earth
3. The earth beneath
4. The water under the earth

Let's define *territorial warfare.* Territorial warfare is to wage war against dark forces by assignment. This assignment is both offensive and defensive. Our defensive assignment in territorial warfare is to know our "area of operation" (or "AO") and to take advantage of the benefits of being in place. In the army, it is not well thought of for one soldier to veer off into another soldier's area of expertise. Every soldier is assigned a MOS (Military Occupation Specialty) when he or she is processed into the army. God gave Joshua a revelation of the benefits of knowing your area of operation in spiritual warfare.

> Every place that the sole of your foot will tread upon I have given you, as I said to Moses. From the wilderness and this Lebanon as far as the great river, the River Euphrates, all the land of the Hittites, and to the Great Sea toward the going down of the sun, shall be your territory. No man shall be able to stand before you all the days of your life; as I was with Moses, so I will be with you. I will not leave you nor forsake you.
>
> —JOSHUA 1:3–5

This scripture tells us the benefits of being in place:

1. Wherever the soles of your feet shall tread, the land will be subdued (according to your territory).

2. No enemy will be able to stand before you, in opposition, all the days of your life.

3. Just as God was with Moses and Joshua, He will be with us.

Wow! What an awesome benefits packet! The natural military never offered me a deal like this. When we go into battle on the Lord's side, we can have the benefits packet of Joshua, and all we have to do is find our area of operation and stay in it. As a sprinter, speed was everything to me. But regardless of speed, if an athlete stepped into another competitor's lane, that person was disqualified. Paul talks about running his own race (2 Tim. 4:7). Your defense in territorial warfare is knowing the perimeters that God has given to you—and not crossing them. Victory will be inevitable!

The offensive assignment of territorial warfare is a piece of cake once you get in place. Just because you are saved does not mean that you are in place. Many Christians live defeated lives and never experience victory in the realm that God designed for them to have it in. Our victory as believers is designated for us in the earth realm. But many focus on the victory they will receive in the heavenly realm after life. God has reserved victory in the heavenly realm for us.

When we have victory in the earth realm, not only do we get something out of it, but God gets what He wants—the glory! God takes pleasure in sitting back on the throne and watching us kick devil butt! I know that these may be strong words, but it's just how I see it.

I imagine that there are spiritual Super Bowl games in heaven where the cloud of witnesses are sitting around cheering for us. One day I was telling God that I wanted to meet some of the people in the Bible. The Holy Spirit cut me off in the middle of my words and said, "There are many in heaven who cannot wait to meet you. They watch your story every day. Your book is at the door!"

I immediately thought that this was a spiritual door and a new book. But when I went to my door, the first copy of my testimony, *Delivered to Destiny,* was literally on my doorstep. This blew my mind, but God wanted me to know that what He had spoken to me was as real as the book at my door.

We are surrounded by a cloud of witnesses (Heb. 12:1). Sometimes I think about how boring it must be for the witnesses of heaven to watch as defeat after defeat and complaint after complaint occurs in our lives. I am sure they "turn their channels" to greater stories about the "forces of the Lord." I know that they do not want to watch as God's people are beaten down repeatedly by a devil that was eternally defeated more than two thousand years ago. As believers, we must stand up and be counted as the forces of the Lord.

Victory in Christ Jesus is not designated only to prayer warriors or to power-packed preachers. Victory is for every believer, but you must mount up and get in place to walk in the offensive assignment of territorial warfare. This is your realm! You are a part of the forces of the Lord, who are a part of the kingdom of God!

We face many challenges in the church, but there are none in the kingdom. The Greek word for *kingdom* is *basilia*. The *basilia* of God is defined as "a realm of total rule and dominion." For this reason, we must walk in an authority that will bring heaven down to earth. This is when the kingdom comes and the will of God is done in the earth realm. We are called to manifest the kingdom in the earth realm.

SPEARHEADING THE ENEMY

A military term for attacking opposition is *spearhead*. To spearhead the enemy is to be a driving force that has the ability to penetrate enemy lines. The term originates from the word *spear*, which is a weapon with a sharp point. A spearhead represents the front forces of a military thrust.

A spearheading force of the Lord abides in a realm where the kingdom suffers violence and takes by force (Matt. 11:12). The power of a spearhead is the force behind it. The word *force* (*harpazo*) in Matthew 11:12 means "to forcibly lay hold of or take possession of." It means "to seize." To *seize* means "to take violently, eagerly, and knowingly." It also means "to have a sudden effect on." When the spearhead of the Lord is released against darkness, God unleashes His faithful forces. They cover every realm that comes up against worship to the Most High God.

THE FORCES OF THE LORD

Let's identify the forces of the Lord.

Foot soldiers (army and marines)

Foot soldiers are the forces of the Lord that have the ability to do hand-to-hand combat. They carry weapons of warfare, but the anointing is in their hands and feet. Psalm 18:34 says that God teaches our hands to do war so that our arms can bend a bow of steel.

The Hebrew word for *hands* is *yad*; it refers to an open hand that is able because of power and dominion. It also means to be consecrated and to be a terror. God's people were considered a terror to their enemies in biblical times. They were feared because of the consecration in which they walked.

The only thing that makes demons tremble in warfare is a person who is holy and separated unto the Lord. Holiness terrorizes darkness! The reason all of the enemies of God feared His people was because He was with them. There was no other reason.

Foot soldiers for Jesus can have the confidence that their enemies will not stand before them, because they are in place and God is with them. People are afraid of demons because they do not have the true presence of God. The real presence of God will make demons afraid of you.

This is why wherever we tread and whatever we put our hands to do prosper. Please understand that this is conditional. First of all, we must remain in our coast or territory. The word *coast* in Joshua 1:4 (KJV) is *gebul* and means "enclosed territory." God gave specific perimeters for where Joshua was to do battle. As long as he stayed within those perimeters, the victory was promised to him. If Joshua stepped out of those perimeters, his *territorial blessing* would become a *territorial curse*.

Outside of the perimeters of God, we are on our own. In our AO, there is a sphere of authority that cannot be denied. The authority of our coast is seated in the soles of our feet. The word *foot* in the first chapter of Joshua is *kaph,* and it means the same as the palm of the hand. Our authority is seated in the center of our hands and feet. When the people went to bury Jezebel, her skull, feet, and the palms of her hands were all that was left (2 Kings 9:35). The word *palms* is this passage is *kaph,* the same as the soles of our feet mentioned in Joshua.

There is one more important fact about foot soldiers to note—they do not just walk; they tread. To tread (*darak*) means "to string a bow and make a path." Foot soldiers are frontline spearheaders. They are apostolic pathfinders and trailblazers who break through in uncharted territories to make a way for the next generation of troops.

Air force

When I was in the military, I often heard this phrase: "Whoever controls the airways rules the land!" In spiritual warfare, air traffic control is very important. God's air force has the ability to control the spiritual airways through the life or death in their tongue. They operate out of the air traffic control tower that God set up in Matthew 18:18–19 (KJV):

> Verily I say unto you, Whatsoever ye shall bind on earth shall be bound in heaven: and whatsoever ye shall loose on earth shall be loosed in heaven. Again I say unto you, That if two of you shall agree on earth as touching any thing that they shall ask, it shall be done for them of my Father which is in heaven.

Pay close attention to the word *touching* in the scripture listed above. It is *peri* in Hebrew, and it means "to form a circuit." There is nothing like the formation of fighter jets that line up to launch attacks against a target. They form a circuit, and in unison they take their enemy out. Though they are all expert fighters in the airways, it is their ability to operate as one force that penetrates their target. They cover each other, because the objective is to hit the target without any casualties.

There are too many casualties of war in the church. God is calling us to use the life and the death of our tongues to control the spiritual airways. The *life of the tongue* gives things permission to exist in the earth realm. The *death of the tongue* forbids things to come into existence or to continue to operate. Many people are ignorant of the powerful weapon of the death of the tongue. It is the weapon that activates the ammunition used to bind.

Nice, religious spirits insist on denying the power that God gave us to take authority over our environment. Those who understand dominion warfare delight in taking over the airways. The air force of the Lord has the authority to say *yea* or *nay* as to what goes on in regions. As we mount up and take our rightful position over the spiritual airways, we will possess the land. When intercession gets to this point, the foot soldiers will not have to work as hard.

The air force of God should be headed by apostles. The Bible says that God put apostles first in spiritual order (1 Cor. 12:28). This word *first* is *proton*, and it means "first in time, place, and order of importance." The order of importance is not that apostles have one thousand churches or that they can preach better than anyone else. The important factor is that apostles have the anointing to set their faces directly against principalities over regions. They are sent ones who have been set in place by God and designated to rule in this realm. When the church gets a better revelation of the End-Time function of the apostle, the foundations of darkness will be shaken from the heavens.

Navy

One day as I was having dinner with Dr. Don Colbert, he mentioned something that helped me to tie some loose ends together in spiritual warfare. Sometimes we do things by the Spirit but have no natural knowledge of why we do them. We must be very careful when we want to know the details of everything. Some things you may just feel right about and may be able to do those things by faith.

One of these things for me was praying by the water. I always felt led to pray by the water. There was no apparent reason other than I just felt led in this direction. Dr. Colbert explained to me about the research done by a group of scientists. These scientists played different kinds of music over containers of water and allowed the water to freeze while the music was playing. When they played demonic music, the water froze with ugly designs in it. On the other hand, when they played praise or positive music, the water froze into the shape of beautiful crystals.

What does this have to do with God's spiritual navy? The results of the scientific testing of the water proved that water carries information. In Genesis 1:2, we know that the earth was without form. The Amplified Version says that it was "an empty waste, and darkness was upon the face of the very great deep." This word *deep* is *tehowm*, and it means "abyss or deep body of water." The Spirit of God *moved* (*rachaph*) on the water. *Rachaph* is described in *Strong's* as "to move and shake."

Water carries information today, because it carried the Word of God in the beginning. Just as there is a natural navy, God has a spiritual navy. This navy guards the waterways.

Submarine

Every navy has a submarine force. The submarine forces of the Lord are specialists. They deal with things that go on in realms that our natural minds cannot fathom. Few people in the church are called to operate in this realm. Dealing with marine, submarine, and water spirits requires opposing high-level witchcraft.

I will not go into the details of this topic in this book. I believe the church is not ready for the reality of what really goes on in the water under the earth. As I mentioned earlier, the strongman of this region is called the queen of the coast. There are people who have considered that they have sold their souls to the devil who would know exactly what I am talking about.

The point I want to make is that this realm does exist. The submarine forces of the Lord are top secret agents who give themselves to the whole truth. They are able to discern both good and evil. They operate on levels in the spirit realm that are subconscious to the general church. They go deeper than what they can understand, and they set their faces against the abominations that go on under the water.

In Hebrews 5:11, Paul said that he really wanted to tell the people in the church more than what he was saying, but he could not do so because they were slothful in spiritual insight. He accused them of becoming addicted to milk. In the sixth chapter of Hebrews, he advised the church to proceed on to advanced teaching.

There is a time for milk, but the general church has been on the bottle so long that the milk has begun to spoil in their bellies. Many church members even want the pastors to warm their milk and feed it to them. We are living in the last days, and men's hearts will fail them for fear because they have been on milk too long. Not everyone is called to deal with the warfare under the water. But on the other hand, there must be an awareness that evil exists in this realm and that it affects the lives of people on earth.

The last realm that I would like to discuss is the one under the earth. The strongman of the underworld is the *queen of hell*. She dispatches orders for the gates of hell from the belly of hell. The Bible encourages us that the gates of hell shall not prevail against the church (Matt. 16:18). These gates are in the core of the earth, and they have portals or vortexes by which demons travel. These gates have keys, and we own them. We have the keys to death, hell, and the grave. This means we have authority over the demonic traffic of the vortexes of hell.

Every believer must be a general enlistee in the Lord's armed forces. God does not take weekend warriors or part-time soldiers. He is not recruiting coast guards to hang out on the edge. He is looking for spiritual "Navy SEALs" who are willing to go out into the deep.

Some people say that it does not take all of this warfare, or that they do not want to get involved in warfare. Let me remind you, there is no demilitarized zone in the spirit! The enemy will not over-look your children because you do not get involved. You are in this battle whether you want to be or not. You are made in the image of God, and every time the devil sees you, he will fight you, if for nothing else than because you remind him of God. Eventually, you will have to fight back or be defeated. Don't attempt to be a solo soldier or a lone ranger. Make a conscious decision to join the forces of the Lord!

FROM A TACTICAL TO A STRATEGIC MIND-SET

To operate in effective warfare in the last days, the church must shift from a tactical to a strategic mind-set. In years past, we have taken a tactical approach to spiritual warfare in the church. To define the word *tactical*, it is important to look at its root word, *tactics*. The definition for *tactics* is "to have skilled methods." The church has depended on the skilled methods of certain headliner individuals in the church to launch attacks against the enemy. This is good to a certain point. We need anointed soldiers on the front lines of ministry to spearhead mighty moves of God. The problem is that the purpose of the spearhead is to make a way for other soldiers to come through.

We really need a revelation of the power of numbers. One soldier can put a thousand to flight (no matter what the rank is). Two soldiers can put ten thousand to flight. (See Deuteronomy 32:30.) An example of a tactical approach in warfare is the soul-winning efforts of one person. One person can only touch so many lives. This person can be gifted and skilled in his or her method, but will be limited in how many people he or she can reach.

Please do not misunderstand my point. We need skilled individuals who are tactical in nature, but this is only the beginning of the overall strategy of God. God's strategy is for us to plan, manage, and direct a joint effort that will be advantageous for the entire body of Christ. We do not have to debate about it, because He laid it out in Ephesians 4:11–15:

> And He Himself gave some to be apostles, some prophets, some evangelists, and some pastors and teachers; for the equipping of the saints for the work of ministry, for the edifying of the body of Christ...that we should no longer be children, tossed to and fro and carried about with every wind of doctrine, by the trickery of men, in the cunning craftiness of deceitful plotting, but, speaking the truth in love, may grow up in all things into Him who is the head—Christ—from whom the whole body, joined and knit together by what every joint supplies, according

to the effective working by which every part does its share, causes growth of the body for the edifying of itself in love.

It is important to note that God has a strategy for His church to fulfill its mission in the earth. All strategies have goals that move toward the maturity of the strategy. God's goal for the church is to equip individual saints unto maturity. The purpose for this equipping is for the work of the ministry. The ultimate goal of the work of the ministry is to edify the entire body of Christ.

A strategic mind-set is an apostolic mind-set. In other words, leaders with apostolic mind-sets are not satisfied with a tactical nature. They are not distracted by the fact that they are gifted and draw crowds by themselves. The heart of a leader with an apostolic mind-set is to incorporate a strategy to multiply his or her gift by training others to do the same thing.

A leader with a tactical mind-set is satisfied with addition only. As long as the ministry is growing, the money is coming in, and the prestige is getting greater, everything is fine with them.

On the other hand, a leader with the strategy of God in his heart seeks multiplication. Addition is not enough! If you add ten plus ten you will come out with twenty. If you multiply ten times ten, you will come out with one hundred. This is how it is in the spirit. God commanded us to be fruitful and multiply. The church has been producing carbon-copy ministries for too long. When another ministry comes along with this pattern, it is not a part of the multiplying plan of God. It is only another addition.

Tactics can be bound by regimen, but strategies take creativity. God is giving His church creative strategies that will call us to be all that we can be. The United States Army has a slogan: "Be all that you can be." Recruiters promise that if you have any potential, the army will pull it out of you.

This is what apostles do. People who have non-apostolic mind-sets travel around only releasing their anointing to people. This is good to a certain point, and I do believe in impartation. But the ultimate goal that

God has for all of His children is that they *be all that He created them to be*. Leaders with apostolic mind-sets have the ability not just to impart what they have to a person, but also to reach on the inside of that person and pull out what God put within before the foundation of the world.

People need more than impartation; they need activation. They need the thing that has been lying dormant in their lives to be turned on. You do not have to be an apostle to activate people into their callings, but you must have an apostolic mind-set. With this mind-set it is hard to limit the "work of the ministry" to our individual churches. It will not even be limited to the work in your city. The strategy of God is for us to hijack regions and nations for the Lord Jesus Christ. Many people have focused on kingdom living, but they have not tapped into kingdom dominion. This takes us outside of our homes, neighborhoods, churches, and cities. Kingdom dominion gives us the nations as our inheritance.

There are many statuses for soldiers in the military. The only status for which soldiers get paid is "active duty military." Soldiers must be activated to receive their military benefits. Many in the body of Christ are not experiencing the benefits of salvation because they have potential that lies dormant in their bellies.

I want to end this chapter with two scriptures that will stir up the potential in your belly to do your part in the kingdom. We learn in Ephesians 4:16 that every saint (soldier) has a part in God's plan for His church. It tells us that when the body is properly connected, each joint supplies to other parts of the body that which brings increase.

> Now to Him who is able to do exceedingly abundantly above all that we ask or think, according to the power that works in us.
> —Ephesians 3:20

> The thief does not come except to steal, and to kill, and to destroy: I have come that they may have life, and that they may have it more abundantly.
> —John 10:10

Both of these scriptures speak of one word, *potential. Potential* is defined as "that which can but has not yet." How much potential has gone to the grave from the body of Christ? Ephesians 3:20 says that God is able to do far above what we can think or ask, but it is conditional. The condition is based on the power that is working in us. It is not based on the power that exists alone, but the power that has been activated from within and is working.

This is when we get the benefits! The word *power* is *dunamis,* and means dynamic power. God has put dynamite in many people who have never been ignited. If it has not been ignited, it is laying dormant. Dormant power gets no results! Only power that is working (or doing something) gives God the ability to do above what we ask or think.

This may be hard for many to imagine, but when we get ignited, it ignites the Holy Ghost. Are you waiting on God to use you? Let me give you a revelation—God is waiting on you. When we fulfill the call of God on our life, it ignites abundant life. It is Jesus' will for us to have abundant life, but John 10:10 teaches that this is conditional also. It says that Jesus came that we might have abundant life. The word *might* is *dunamai,* and it means potential. Jesus gave us the potential, and what we do with it determines the kind of life we live.

Abundant life is *perissos* in the Greek language, and it means to live a violent, excessive, superabundant life. God has not called us to haphazardly survive. He has called us to strive and be full of *perissos*! The potential is on the inside of you, but you must be properly connected and activated. Even if you are full of power, if you are not plugged into your place in the body of Christ it will only lie dormant.

As we finish this chapter, pray with me:

> *In the name of Jesus, I come in agreement with what I just read. I transition from a tactical position in the spirit to a strategic one. Father, I thank You for divine alignment and proper placement in the body of Christ, so that my spiritual, physical, mental, emotional, and financial needs will be supplied.*

I speak to anything that God has called me to do that is lying dormant in my life. Faith comes by hearing the Word, and I have heard the words of this chapter. I will not just be a hearer, but a doer of what I have read. The potential of God on the inside of me and those whom I am called to influence will not go to the grave. It will do what God has called it to do in the earth realm.

Father, I thank You for making my personal assignment in the body clear to me. From this point forward, I am an active duty soldier in the army of the Lord. All the benefits that have been held back up to this time will be returned unto me sevenfold. I receive my back pay according to Proverbs 6:31 now, in Jesus' name!

Congratulations! You have been activated in the army of the Lord!

CHAPTER SIXTEEN

Breaking the Power of Vicious Cycles

Cutting the Enemy Off at the Root

INTENTIONALLY LEFT THIS topic for the last chapter of this book. If you have completed the earlier chapters, you have been taken to new levels in God in spiritual warfare. This chapter will assist you in dealing with backlash, retaliation, and revenge from the enemy.

It is very important to understand how to break vicious cycles. Many people live under the power of recurring attacks and never take authority over them. This chapter will help you to cut the attacks of the enemy off at the root.

Ephesians 2:2 (AMP) reads:

> In which at one time you walked [habitually]. You were following the course and the fashion of this world [were under the sway of the tendency of this present age], following the prince of the power of the air. [You were obedient to and under the control of] the [demon] spirit that still constantly works in the sons

of disobedience [the careless, the rebellious, and the unbelieving, who go against the purposes of God].

Many would argue that this scripture is only speaking of the people of the world. I beg to differ. Because it addresses the careless, rebellious, and the unbelieving, I have to take the opposite position. There are too many people in the church who fall into these categories. I do agree that Paul is addressing someone who used to be in this state, but my objective is to address those who are still struggling!

Paul mentions a habitual course. To get people off of habitual courses, we must break vicious cycles. You may be a minister who is trying to break an addiction, or a businessman who cannot overcome thoughts of suicide. No matter who you are or what you struggle with, this chapter is the answer to your prayers.

An important part of intercession is breaking up fallow ground so that people can be made free. This work should be done before a deliverance or counseling session. So many people are working overtime in setting captives free because no one has paid the price in prayer. The strongholds of the enemy must be penetrated before they can be pulled down. Imaginations must be cast down before strongholds are penetrated.

Strongholds are made up of imaginations. Intercession must be done on the behalf of bound individuals before they have the ability to cast down imaginations. Intercession breaks up the fallow ground of the mind of the individual before the actual ministry begins.

To break up the fallow ground means to till the concentration of bondage that has set in. The fallow ground has to be broken up in the minds of preachers who are addicted to pornography, or in deacons who molest boys in the church. These seem like unthinkable things for people in these positions to do. But these kinds of sins happen because the people are bound by vicious cycles.

The sad part is that they are part of something that is so much greater than their own personal problem. A deacon may molest boys in the church because he was molested as a boy in the same church. A preacher may be bound by pornographic material because his daddy was in the ministry and did the same thing.

We have been taught about generational curses, but vicious cycles go deeper. They do not just run in the bloodline. It is a kind of transference of spirits that does not need a family line to flow through. The legal right of vicious cycles is through association. The word *associate* means "to connect or touch in some way."

The name of the demon that transfers spirits is Azazel, a desert spirit in the Old Testament. It was called the scapegoat.

> Aaron shall cast lots on the two goats—one lot for the Lord, the other lot for Azazel or removal. And Aaron shall bring one goat on which the Lord's lot fell and offer him as a sin offering. But the goat on which the lot fell for Azazel or removal shall be presented alive before the Lord to make atonement over him, that he may be let go into the wilderness for Azazel (for dismissal).
> —LEVITICUS 16:8–10, AMP

The term *scapegoat* is taken from this scripture, but the meaning of the word is "to take the blame." The sins of the people, via the goat, were sent to the desert to Azazel for their atonement. The (sins) spirits were transferred.

Hollywood took note of this principle in the movie *The Fallen*, where Denzel Washington played the lead character. A demon called *Azazel* transferred from person to person whenever the person with the spirit made contact with another person. This spirit transferred through generations even though there was no family association. Sin is contagious, and in many occult environments this is called *contagious magic*. I call them vicious cycles!

Just as in Ephesians 2:2, people are bound under a sway or tendency, and they are not even aware of it. Though we must do the ground-level warfare of casting devils out, the power of the sway and tendency must be broken. People must be disconnected from the power of the air. Christians and nonbelievers alike are bound this way. If Christians operate in rebellion, carelessness, or unbelief, they will reap the fruit of the seeds they have planted. Scripture is clear on this:

> Do not be deceived, God is not mocked; for whatever a man sows, that he will also reap.
>
> —GALATIANS 6:7

How do we intercede for people under the power of vicious cycles? One approach is to curse the spirit of Azazel to the root and send it to the desert. Matthew 12:43 teaches that demons seek dry places after they are cast out. This word is *anudros* in the Greek. It refers to water-less (spiritless) places in a person that would make room for devils to reenter them. In the case of Azazel, *send him to the desert!* He needs the next body to thrive in, and in the spiritual desert to which we send him, there is no human life. His cycle will be cursed to the root.

CURSES MUST BE DEALT WITH AT THE ROOT

In Mark 11:21, Jesus cursed the fig tree to the root. It was not doing what it was called to do. Rebellion is the same as the sin of witchcraft. Witchcraft comes up against the truth, and it will infiltrate the lives of believers if lines are crossed.

No, the devil cannot cross the lines drawn by the blood of Jesus, but we can! Ecclesiastes 10:8 says that whoever breaks through a hedge will be bitten by a serpent. We cannot cross over into the enemy's territory and think we will be covered. Be not deceived about what is enemy territory. Enemy territory is any place that you attempt to walk outside of the will of God. Remember this—if God did not send you, you are on your own, and the enemy has legal right to deal with you as he pleases.

Even when you are operating in your assigned territory, always pay close attention to detail. The enemy does not play by the rules. If Lucifer rebelled against God in heaven, he may not have a lot of respect for you in your house or your church. You must make him respect you! The enemy respects authority and discernment. When you have both of these flowing in your life, it terrorizes darkness.

Saul initiated his rebellion by disobedience to God in the small things. This act ultimately led him to consult familiar spirits. The little foxes spoil the entire vine (Song of Sol. 2:15), and a little leaven leavens the whole lump (1 Cor. 5:6). Achan disobeyed God, and it allowed a little nation called Ai to cause Joshua and his champion army to fall. (See Joshua 7.) Achan, his family, and all of his possessions were burned (cursed) to the root. This is called *spiritual cauterization*. It occurs when you burn and seal the power of the curse.

Dealing With Demonic Hydras

The ultimate warfare tactic in dealing with a vicious cycle is breaking the power of the hydra. When I first started doing spiritual warfare, the Lord prompted my heart to understand that witchcraft and recurring attacks needed to be burned to the root. Before I was saved I was fascinated with Greek mythology.

Many years ago, God brought to my memory the Greek myth about Hercules and the hydra. I began breaking the power of the hydra when I was engaged in warfare prayer. Though the hydra is said to be a mythological creature, I know it to be a spirit that must be dealt with to break vicious cycles.

Recently I heard Bishop Tutor Bismark mention the hydra in one of his services. I was surprised, because I had never heard a preacher mention the hydra. God stirred my heart to look deeper into the revelation of the hydra so that intercessors would know how to break the power of recurring curses.

Hercules was assigned to fight this hideous creature with nine heads. Every time Hercules cut off one head of the monster, two more heads would grow out of the place where one used to be. This represents demonic multiplication of problems. Can you imagine getting rid of one problem, and in that same place where it used to reside, two similar problems are immediately birthed?

The real problem with the witchcraft of the spirit of the hydra is that the problems occur with a domino affect. No one involved ever gets a break. The goal of hydra witchcraft is to wear you out. When people get weary, they break down.

I also found out that a hydra is a type of sea monster and a constellation in the sky. This means that we have to deal with hydras under the water and hydras in the air. So how do we begin to deal with nine-headed problems that come at us from every direction? We do it one head at a time!

Each head of the hydra represents something. If you will burn each head at the root of the situation you are dealing with, you will be guaranteed victory in this area.

The nine heads of the hydra

1. *The unity of evil alliances must be destroyed.* Confusion and division must be sent against the works and plans of the enemy. In Genesis 11:4, God sent confusion to stop the evil plans of the people at the Tower of Babel. There were also many other times that God sent confusion to the enemy's camp on behalf of His people.

2. *Destroy the demonic double portion.* The demonic double portion is explained in Matthew 23:15. This passage says that some religious people search high and low to win one convert to Christ. After they win the person to Christ, they cause that person to be doubly as hellish as they are. The demonic double portion is rooted in people who pretend to be in Christ, but are evil. Recognize who is being used by this spirit, and deal with it. One of the most common arrows against saints is "friendly fire." These arrows come from those to whom we open ourselves and trust.

The sixteenth chapter of Judges says that the lords of the Philistines paid Delilah to entice Sampson. This particular word, *entice*, means "to open up mentally and morally." In order for the arrows of evil people to affect us, we have to open ourselves up to them. It is an inside job.

3. *Three is representative of the trinity. The demonic trinity is called a type of threefold cord.* There are also godly threefold cords. In dealing with the third head of the hydra, we must break the connection of all demonic threefold cords. Ecclesiastes 4:12 states threefold cords are not easily broken. Disallow this connection. Demons gain power by groupings. Sever their alliance, and they are helpless.

4. *Job 38:12–13 teaches that we can command the morning so that the dayspring will know its place and wickedness will be shaken out of the four corners of the heavens.* In dealing with the fourth head of the hydra, wickedness must be shaken out of the four corners of the earth concerning what you are dealing with. In this kind of warfare, we deal in the heavens, for as I mentioned earlier, one kind of hydra is a group of stars or a constellation.

5. *The number five is the number for grace.* When you are dealing with the fifth head of the hydra, you must come against demonic grace. Cauterize any place, time, or favor that darkness may be causing to work against you. In Psalm 41:10–11, the psalmist prayed, "Be merciful to me, and raise me up, that I may repay them. By this I know that You are well pleased with me, because my enemy does not triumph over me."

Curse the favor of demonic assignments to the root. Declare the enemies' efforts favorless, and his attempts will be fruitless.

6. *On the sixth day, the Lord finished the work. The counterfeit of this principle is the finished work of darkness.* Bind up the finished work of the things working against you! Declare that your enemy shall not finish and that his work will be an open mockery.

7. *Seven is representative of a day of rest.* I was once praying for a young man, and the demon spoke through the young man saying, "You have awakened me!" Demons desire to take up resting places in our circumstances and situations. Prophesy spiritual insomnia against your enemies. Every sleeping giant that is working against you must wake up and be tormented when you deal with the seventh head of the hydra. Give your enemies no room to rest!

8. *Eight is the number of new beginnings.* The eighth head of the hydra is very important. This head gives all the other heads the ability to reproduce through the anointing of *new beginnings.* This is how a new head continues to grow every time one is cut off. There is a demonic new beginning, and it must be cauterized. When you have dealt with the eighth head of the hydra, you will experience less backlash, retaliation, and revenge of the enemy.

9. *Nine is the number for new birth.* The power of the hydra's ability to give birth must be destroyed. Pray for spiritual abortion and miscarriage so that the enemy's plans will not be carried full term. A name

for a demonic baby is a *cambion*. It is the seed of Satan. Curse the cambion to the root before it is birthed, and it will never come into existence. The fertility of the reproductive organs of the ninth head will become barren.

PRAYER FOR BREAKING VICIOUS CYCLES

Father, I thank You that the power of every recurring curse is broken. I curse the spirit of Azazel and send it to the desert. You will not transfer again. You will not transfer through generations, associations, or incantations. I burn and seal your assignment in the name of Jesus.

I plead the blood over the minds of every person involved. I command the fallow ground of their hearts and minds to be broken up. I pull every root from the ground that would cause the curse to spread under the ground. I sever the alliance of the enemy's unity, and I send dissention, confusion, and mutiny to the enemy's camp.

Let there be no agreement in the strongman of the cycle's house. I decree and declare that the demonic double portion shall not manifest. Let the demonic anointing of the vicious cycle decrease until it is dried up. The threefold cord of the cycle is disconnected. Let breaches and gaps be in their midst.

I shut down the authority of the demons that send false winds from the four corners of the earth. Let the ruwach *of God overtake them. With death in my tongue, I say that there is no grace for the enemies that oversee this curse. Demonic grace is bound, and there shall be no time, resources, or favor that will work against the will of God.*

The finished work of the cycle shall never be completed. I speak incompletion, deficiency, shortcoming, immaturity, wanting, and failure of that which would attempt to keep it stirring.

I command the whirlwind that reinforces the cycle to be sucked back into the vortex from which it came.

I declare that the strongman and imps that are assigned to the cycle will have no rest. There will be no new beginning or new birth. I curse the matrix of the cycle and declare its womb barren. Every head of the hydra is cauterized above the earth and under the water. Let the skyline over the waters be covered with the blood of Jesus, so that the air hydras and water hydras will have no agreement in the earth realm. In Jesus' name I pray. Amen.

The Sperm
of the Word

When anyone hears the word of the kingdom, and does not understand it, then the wicked one comes and snatches away what was sown in his heart. This is he who received seed by the wayside.

—MATTHEW 13:19

THIS SCRIPTURE TELLS of the parable of the sower. The Bible says that the person in this passage heard the Word of God but did not understand it. This word *understand* is *suniemi*, and it means to be wise with what is heard and take consideration of it.

Because this person did not take consideration of what he heard, the wicked one took what was sown. The seed of the Word was never planted, so there was no growth. Believers must get a revelation of the seed of the Word. This is what the enemy is after. The personal visions, dreams, and prophecies that God gives to us are like eggs waiting to be fertilized. The seed or *sperma* (spiritual sperm) of the Word must fertilize these dreams, visions, and prophecies for conception to take place.

Matthew 13:24 tells us that the kingdom of heaven is like a man who sows good seed in his field. It goes on to say that while the man slept, his enemy came in and sowed bad seed in the same field.

When the bad seed sprang up, the man was baffled as to how he could sow good seed and end up with bad seed in the midst of it. The word *seed* is *sperma,* and it represents a release of the seed. I call it a spermatic word!

We must also take a look at another Greek word for seed, and it is *spiero. Spiero* means "received seed." *Spiero* is related to the word *spiral,* because it sucks in that which is released to receive it. It is easy to figure out that the seed of the Word must be released and received for conception to take place. A vision that is not conceived will eventually die out from warfare. Another word for *conceive* is *to comprehend* or to be able to imagine. Many confess the Word of God but cannot really imagine the things that they speak out of their mouth.

You really have to be able to see or picture what you are believing God for. If you cannot see it, you will not achieve it. This is spiritual conception. The picture of your promise has to be as real to you as looking into the mirror. It is hard to stop a man who can see what he believes!

The devil comes immediately to do everything in his ability to stop us from imagining the promises of God. The church does not talk enough about positive imagination. These are images in our minds that draw us into our destiny. When I was a sprinter, I used to run my race over and over again in my mind. By the time I stood at the starting line, I had won my race a thousand times. I could visualize my victory, and it boosted my confidence. As intercessors we must be able to see the things that we are believing God for. We must see for ourselves and for others for whom we are called to stand in the gap.

Spermalogos is another Greek word for seed. It is a kind of tare. A tare is a weed that eventually chokes out the real seed. It is the counterfeit to the *sperma* of the Word. It goes into the ground just like a regular seed. You cannot tell that it is a weed until it sprouts. Behind the scenes (underground) it maneuvers to choke the life out of the genuine seed. This is why the man in the parable was surprised that he had weeds in the midst of his seed. When true seed is planted, it brings forth fruit that is pleasing to God. This fruit speaks life.

The fruit of *spermalogos* is trifling talk, gossip, and words that take away from the vision of God. The fruit of *spermalogos* is also superficial, shallow, frivolous, idle, and foolish. We must be watchful of the kind of seeds that we plant in our prayer lives. Bad seed will choke the good seed out. Remember, whatever is sown will be grown. Protect your spiritual garden from the curse of *spermalogos*. The enemy comes so quickly to steal the Word of God that he gets it at its seed stage. The prosperity of the Lord is to reap from what has been sown. If you are sowing and not reaping, an enemy is somewhere behind the scenes destroying your increase.

GETTING PAST GAZA

The ultimate joy of the devil is to destroy our seed. It is a terrible thing to sow and not reap. This is the fruit of the spirit of poverty. In Judges 6:3, the Bible says that every time the people of Israel sowed their seed, the Midianites destroyed their increase. They left no nourishment for the people of Israel. This passage specifically says that their increase could only be destroyed as far as Gaza. People of God, to experience true prosperity, *we must get past Gaza*! Your seed is precious, and this is why the devil comes immediately to steal it. He is a seedeater. His goal is to destroy the seed, because without it you will always be in need. Where there is no seed, there is no multiplication.

The good news is that the enemy has limitations. In this case, it was a place called Gaza. Gaza means "the place of the strong will," and it is a territorial spirit. Territorial spirits are limited to jurisdiction of authority based on territory. If you can get past their jurisdiction of authority, they have no rule over you. You have to get past Gaza. It is like getting past a county line where the laws are different. When you get past Gaza, spiritual law overrides the enemy's right to destroy your increase. Though Gaza is a natural place, it represents a place in the spirit.

Judges 6:6 speaks of the great poverty of Israel. The spirit of poverty is a curse, and it must be broken off of God's people. As I mentioned earlier, there are too many needy intercessors. We all have needs, and it is the will of the Father to meet them. The need that I am referring to is a *spirit of need*. This means that there is a demon that keeps people in constant want to the point that they are distracted from their purpose. Need that distracts you from your purpose is demonic and should not be tolerated.

The Israelites cried out to God for deliverance. Because poverty is a spirit, the people that are bound by it must be delivered. Poverty is a mind-set. The strength of poverty is not the manifestations, but what is actually happening behind the scenes. Poverty does not just grip pockets; it grips the mind.

Judges 6:15 tells us that Gideon's family was the poorest in Israel, yet God chose him to lead his people out of bondage. Gideon had to get past the circumstances that were before him. To be delivered from poverty, he had to change his way of thinking. This was his spiritual barrier, or Gaza. The enemy can only bind you up as far as your mind will limit you.

In doing research, I discovered that Gaza is currently one of the most poverty-stricken places in the world. Scripture declares that God cursed the land of Gaza to be bald. The Philistines were trading His people as slaves, and God pronounced eternal judgment upon them. Today the curse is so prevalent that people cannot get jobs there. Gaza is located between Egypt and Israel. Still today, anyone born in Gaza is not allowed entrance to Israel. They have to remain in Gaza or go to Egypt.

I believe there is a spiritual meaning to this. Though Gaza is between Egypt and Israel in the natural, spiritual Gaza is set up the same. Egypt represents the world, Israel represents the Promised Land, and Gaza is a type of wilderness in the spirit. All believers have an Egypt that they have come out of, but they must go through Gaza to get to their Jerusalem in the spirit.

Even though you may be having a Gaza experience as you have

read this book, move forward and get past it. You must get past Gaza! If you stay where you are, the enemy has the right to destroy your increase.

Samson was a Nazirite separated unto the Lord, but he lost his anointing in Gaza. It all started when he went into the harlot in Gaza. His parents warned him not to indulge himself with foreign women. Soon after that he fell in love with another woman in Gaza, Delilah. By the doors opened in this relationship, he was bound, blinded, and sent to prison; he ultimately died in Gaza. Gaza is known as the place of the uncircumcised. Be circumcised and separated unto the Lord. Allow the Lord to keep you and your children from the accursed thing.

In closing, I would like to emphasize that during the time that Israel was in great poverty, God sent a prophet to them. The prophet reminded them that God had brought them out of Egypt (Judg. 6:8). Gideon asked God that if He was with them, then why were bad things befalling them? He asked, "Where are the miracles that our fathers told us about?" He even asked, "Did the Lord really bring us out of Egypt as our fathers have told?"

Prophet of God, are you reminded of what God has brought you out of up to this point in your life? No matter what you have experienced, never forget the goodness of the Lord. He has already done great things for you. Do not allow your present situation to rob you of what God has already done. Be thankful. A prayerful heart is a thankful heart.

We cannot enter into God's gates for anything without first thanking Him for what He has already done. Build a memorial for you and your family, and dedicate it to the blessings of the Lord. Rehearse them with your children so that they will never question the blessings and deliverance of the Lord. Keep notes of the miracles that God manifests in your everyday life, and pass them down through your generations. This will empower your bloodline to serve the Lord wholeheartedly, in the good times and the bad.

I speak blessings over everything you put your hands to the plow to do according to the will of God. Read the prayers throughout this book (aloud) on behalf of your family. I fertilize your seed with blessings and declare that the mouth of the devourer is shut forever against you and your generations.

I'm outta here!

—Apostle Kim

THE GAZA PRAYER

I set my face against the territorial spirit of Gaza and the things that keep me in battle because the enemy will not release them. The "place of the strong will" is destroyed! I am a sheep and not a goat. I am anointed to follow God wholeheartedly.

I call the rebuke of the Lord upon the devourers set against me. I take authority over the earth and prophesy to her womb to yield increase to me. I declare spiritual, physical, mental, emotional, and material nourishment to replace any malnourished areas of my life and the life of my seed. I speak to the spirit of slack and command it to tighten up so that the standard of God may be raised.

I prophesy to everything that is dull and unfinished and command it to shine and be complete. I command the slow to be quickened by the set timing of God. I resist the children of the east, and say that they will not devour my blessings. I destroy every self-built stronghold in my life with the death of my tongue. May it become a stepping-stone to my next level.

I prophesy to the thin and command it to be fat. I speak life to the failing and undone and command it to be transformed into that which will cause me to hear, understand, and declare the will of the Lord. I release life with my tongue. I prophesy to darkness and command the light to come. I prophesy to everything that is empty in my life and command it to become full.

I prophesy to the dead and say live! I prophesy to that which is held down and oppressed and declare that it shall rise now. I prophesy to that which has been held back and put pressure on it to come forth. Daw lal (spirit of poverty), I command you to be transformed into bool *(prosperity) right now, in Jesus' name.*

A Prayer for Your Seed

I repent for my sins and any iniquities of my past or present that may work against the lives of my children in a negative fashion. I call out my children by name. [Name each child aloud.] I thank You for the salvation, healing, deliverance, and prosperity of my children.

Let every hidden thing operating behind the scenes be exposed by the spotlight of the Holy Ghost. I command every generational sin to be disconnected from my bloodline, in Jesus' name! I curse every demon to the root that transferred through the umbilical cord, and I plead the blood over the navel(s) of my children. The blessings shall flow through their lineage, and the curses are blocked and bound. Every destiny devourer is cut off from my seed.

My seed shall live and fulfill the perfect will of God in the earth. The power of peer pressure and ungodly association is broken. It is replaced by the pressure of the Holy Ghost and closer relationship with God. My children are not bound by the spirit of the world. All fetishes hiding behind fads are exposed and renounced. Every vicious cycle ruling over my seed by association, incantation, or generation is destroyed by the whirlwind of the Lord. All word curses spoken ignorantly or intentionally are cut off from my children forever.

I close every illegitimate door that has been opened against them now. Uncommon favor and doors that the Lord has ordained are wide open. I call all demonic seeds, plans, nightmares, omens, and false visions that have been assigned in the dream lives of my children to dry up. I plead the blood of Jesus over my children wherever they sleep. Incubus, Succubus, spirits of molestation, masturbation, and all other perverse acts are far from them. My seed is holy, separated unto the Lord, and cannot be contaminated by darkness.

Rebellion and disobedience shall not rule over my seed.

Sickness and disease shall not rule over my seed. Poverty and lack shall not rule over my seed. My seed has victory over death, hell, and the grave. The words of this prayer are programmed in the heavens forever! Amen.

Notes

Chapter 3
Putting Your Finger on the Enemy

    1. Kimberly Daniels, *Clean House, Strong House* (Lake Mary, FL: Charisma House, 2003).

Chapter 5
Maneuvering in the Spirit

    1. Kimberly Daniels, *Delivered to Destiny* (Lake Mary, FL: Charisma House, 2004).

Chapter 14
Spiritual Authority in the Army of the Lord (Part 2)

    1. Apostle John Eckhardt has published a great book, titled *Marine Demons*, that talks about marine spirits, available at www.impactnetwork .net or by calling the Crusaders' Ministries office at 708-922-0983.

Kick the enemy to the curb once and for all!

Apostle Kim Daniels has a powerful deliverance ministry, and she could change your life forever. Here are three more road maps to victory.

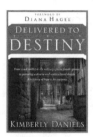

"Experience the deliverance for yourself."

Fasten your seat belts and step into this woman's world whose life reads like a movie script. From witchcraft, drugs, and prostitution to international speaker and pastor, God has had a powerful presence in her life.

978-1-59185-614-6 / $13.99

Put the squeeze on Satan!

You don't have to live in oppression, addiction, or any kind of bondage. You can get rid of those pesky problems of habitual sins today.

978-0-88419-964-9 / $13.99

Recognize the enemy's traps in the church!

Pastor Kim Daniels exposes the snakes in the pews that prevent believers from experiencing a truly transformed life in Christ

978-0-88419-935-9 / $12.99

Visit your local bookstore.